SKI TOWN
SHENANIGANS

THE BEST OF
THE STEAMBOAT SPRINGS
POLICE BLOTTER

· · · · · · · · · · · · · · · · · · · ·

Compiled by Matt Stensland
Designed by Veronika Khanisenko
Illustrated by Mack Maschmeier

D0167422

Acknowledgments

This book would not have been possible without local law enforcement and the support
of the following businesses:
All That, The Core, Hayden Mercantile, Lyon Drug, Off the Beaten Path bookstore,
Retreatia.com, Space Station, The Steamboat Group, Steamboat Ski and Resort Corp.,
Steamboat Treasures & Tees, Straightline Sports, Walgreens and Wild Plum.

We would also like to thank Bert Hull and his staff at Sunflower Publishing for
consulting on this book.

Designed, illustrated, edited and compiled by staff at the Steamboat Pilot & Today.

9   8   7   6   5   4   3   2   1

ISBN 978-0-692-44480-1
Printing services by Sunflower Publishing in Lawrence, Kansas
Typeset in Abadi MT Condensed Light and Alexandria FLF

Library of Congress Control Number 2015908029

Steamboat Pilot & Today
1901 Curve Plaza
PO Box 774827
Steamboat Springs, CO 80477

www.skitownshenanigans.com
www.steamboattoday.com
Find the Steamboat Springs Police Blotter and Steamboat Pilot & Today on Facebook.

Preface

One day in the newsroom, it became clear we were facing a crisis.

No, the dam did not break, and the bears were behaving. No Russian soldiers could be seen parachuting into the Yampa Valley.

What we faced was far more serious. Our best police blotter entries were wasting away in bound volumes in the archive room, otherwise known as the newspaper morgue.

Something had to be done.

People were forgetting about the numerous times men were observed running through the streets and hotel hallways wearing nothing but a thong. Our local police force also once tried to help a drunken Steamboat visitor find his lost monkey.

And who could forget about all those blotter entries involving the local, mostly harmless black bear population? Bears learning how to open the doors on Subarus and destroying the interiors. Bears discovered in homes munching on pistachios and peanut butter. Bears trying to hibernate for the winter under vacation home hot tubs.

Then there is the gem from 2007, when a woman was stuck in her car because a bear was "staring at her from the woods."

While scavenging through 10 years of police blotter entries, it quickly became clear that people will call cops for any reason. Local police get called to help change smoke detector batteries. They get called because a man found a beer bottle in his yard. They get called because a basset hound crashed a wedding reception at the Steamboat Springs Community Center.

As the cliche goes, you can't make this stuff up.

When I tell people I work at the Steamboat Pilot & Today, they usually ask if I am the guy who writes the police blotter. "Yup, that's me, five days a week," I respond. They react as though they are meeting a celebrity.

I take pride in my work, and it's great when I meet blotter fans, but it troubles me when people only remember parts of their favorite police calls.

"I love the one about the girl being chased down the mountain by a giraffe," one woman told me.

She did not remember the rest of the details. Something had to be done.

A police blotter is published in many small-town newspapers and serves numerous roles. Sure, there is some entertainment value, but it also informs the curious about why there were cops in their neighborhood. It helps the community know about crime trends and can help prevent crime.

It is important for people to understand that the police blotter is not meant to just make people laugh, and this book is not meant to marginalize our local police. We have to remember that the people calling for help are sometimes having the worst day of their lives. But in this book, we chose to primarily focus on the calls that make people laugh.

Many ask how we compile the police blotter, which appears daily in the newspaper as "The Record."

Every day at 7 a.m., we get an email that contains all the calls from the previous day. We get the time, location and nature of each call. Then we call the officers and fire chiefs about the calls, trying not to take more than 10 minutes of their time, which we value. We follow up on more serious incidents for stories and write summaries of the rest of the calls in the blotter.

The Steamboat Pilot has been publishing the local news since 1885, and in August 2014, the Steamboat Today celebrated its 25th anniversary of publishing a daily newspaper. It was a proud moment, and we look forward to continuing to report on important news, issues and our ski town shenanigans.

Matt Stensland
Cops and courts reporter

· · · · · · · · 2005 · · · · · · · ·

Sept. 21

11:28 p.m. Several people reportedly were sliding down stair railings with a kayak in the 1300 block of Bob Adams Drive. Officers did not contact the people because the activity is not illegal.

Jan. 6

1:42 a.m. Extra patrol was requested to help find a 22-year-old man who escaped from the back of a police patrol car in Ski Time Square. The man was found 12 hours later in his home on Pine Street and arrested on suspicion of drunken driving and escaping police.

• • • • • • • • • • • • • • • •

Jan. 9

4:32 a.m. A man reported hearing noises on his roof in the 400 block of Locust Court. The man said it had been going on for 45 minutes and sounded louder than noises an animal would make. The police investigated and found no tracks on the roof and surmised it to be melting or falling snow.

• • • • • • • • • • • • • • • •

Jan. 11

9:27 p.m. A 21-year-old man was arrested at the Musicfest Tent for disorderly conduct, third-degree trespassing and possession of drug paraphernalia. He reportedly was asked to leave a concert for being rowdy. He left but then returned.

• • • • • • • • • • • • • • • •

Jan. 12

9:34 p.m. Two 16-year-old runway juveniles from Cheyenne, Wyo., were found in a condo belonging to the father of one of the boys in the 1900 block of Ski Time Square Drive. More than $500 worth of stolen ski and snowboard merchandise also was found inside the condo.

• • • • • • • • • • • • • • • •

Jan. 13

6:46 a.m. Someone reportedly drove a vehicle around the rodeo grounds illegally, got stuck and then left the vehicle there. The vehicle was towed, and the driver was issued a citation.

Jan. 15

8:26 p.m. An officer was requested in the 1500 block of Meadow Lane to respond to a suspicious incident. A woman saw someone taking photographs of her home. The photographer turned out to be a neighbor documenting code violations.

• • • • • • • • • • • • • • • •

Jan. 19

5:28 p.m. Two mattresses reportedly were on fire in a pile of rubbish in the 1300 block of Dream Island Mobile Home Park.

11:33 p.m. As police were responding to a loud party in the 700 block of Walton Pond Circle, a 21-year-old man took one of the police officer's flashlights and tried to hide it behind his back. The man was arrested for theft and obstructing government operations.

• • • • • • • • • • • • • • • •

Jan. 20

9:52 a.m. Theft was reported in the 900 block of Lincoln Avenue. The reporting party alleged that a man was charging people rent to use a cluster mailbox owned by the U.S. Postal Service. Investigation of the incident was handed over to the U.S. Postal Inspector.

9:35 p.m. Troopers pulled over a Denver-area woman on Rabbit Ears Pass for a traffic violation. They called police after they found a large number of condoms in her car, a recent check-in receipt from a Steamboat hotel and a how-to pamphlet that led them to suspect she was a prostitute. Police were unable to charge her because they were unable to locate the man involved in the alleged incident.

• • • • • • • • • • • • • • • •

Jan. 22

7:07 p.m. Deputies responded to a wildlife call on Routt County Road 27 near Oak Creek, where a caller reported an injured raccoon, possibly with broken legs, in the road. The deputy couldn't locate the raccoon.

3:29 a.m. A man who had parked his 1989 Jeep Wagoneer in the parking garage under Torian Plum Plaza reported that his vehicle was stolen. The keys were left in the center console. The Jeep was quickly found in Ski Time Square across from Dos Amigos restaurant. A 12-pack of Budweiser was in the front seat.

Feb. 2

Jan. 22

8:38 p.m. Steamboat Springs police responded to a report of a stolen vehicle at Sheraton Steamboat Resort. According to police, an unidentified suspect stole a red Toyota Highlander from a hotel guest when the suspect pretended to be a hotel employee. The guest gave the vehicle to the suspect, who the guest thought was a valet parking attendant. About 18 hours after checking in, the guest requested his vehicle, which hotel employees said they knew nothing about. The theft was then reported to police.

. . . .

Jan. 25

2:00 p.m. Two people in the 100 block of Hillside Drive refused to return a UPS package that was wrongly delivered to their residence. The package contained a toy hovercraft. The people reportedly told the UPS man asking for the package back, "finders keepers, losers weepers."

Jan. 31

8:13 p.m. A report was made that someone had been throwing snowballs at vehicles on Burgess Creek Road for three nights in a row.

. . . .

Feb. 3

11:26 a.m. An officer was requested for a highly intoxicated man who had come into the emergency room at Yampa Valley Medical Center to visit his ex-wife. The man refused to leave the ER and mistakenly took a woman's diaper bag instead of his backpack.

. . . .

Feb. 9

10:47 a.m. A manager at a hotel in the 3100 block of Ingles Lane reported to police that a guest had backed up the toilet, and it was leaking onto the floor.

. . . .

Feb. 15

3:18 a.m. A woman reported that cash had been stolen from her residence in the 3200 block of Après Ski Way. It later was discovered that no cash was stolen and that the woman just wanted to talk to someone.

. . . .

Feb. 16

7:47 p.m. A person reported hearing screaming and hollering in the 3000 block of Village Drive. It turned out to be a family having a playful wrestling match.

. . . .

Feb. 17

8:35 p.m. A woman called police worried that her daughter was hanging out with illegal immigrants and doing drugs. The woman had questions for police about the situation.

12:47 p.m. Vandalism was reported in the 1000 block of Merritt Street. Someone put dog poop in a paper bag, lit it on fire, left it on someone's doorstep and rang the doorbell. The homeowner didn't fall for the prank.

March 11

Feb. 20

7:00 a.m. An intoxicated man was reported in the 700 block of Lincoln Avenue. He apparently had slept outside all night and was suffering from hypothermia. The man was taken by ambulance to the hospital.

. . . .

Feb. 21

1:30 a.m. A woman in the 1400 block of Blue Sage Drive called police fearing there was an intruder in her home. The woman said she heard a vehicle leaving and a sound like a snowblowing machine. Police investigated and discovered the woman's significant other made the sounds.

Feb. 23

12:14 p.m. A suspicious incident was reported in the 2500 block of Ski Trail Lane. The reporting party said she owned a rental unit and was calling on behalf of her tenant, who suspected someone was staying in the unit when she went out of town because she found black hairs in the bed. The reporting party was concerned about the management of the unit.

. . . .

Feb. 25

12:39 p.m. The Yampa Valley Regional Airport was briefly evacuated after security officials saw what looked like a grenade while scanning carry-on luggage. The item was a belt buckle designed to look like a grenade. Its owner was cooperative with police.

. . . .

Feb. 28

12:52 a.m. A report was made that a young man carrying a street sign had yelled at another man that he was going to kill him in his sleep in the 2400 block of Après Ski Way. Police found the man with a "no parking" sign and arrested him after a short foot chase. The 24-year-old man was arrested on suspicion of criminal mischief and theft.

9:42 p.m. A man complained that trash was being dumped in a hot tub in the 1600 block of Shadow Run Frontage. He complained about parties in the area and, that the hot tub was so trashed that someone had to dump out all the water and redo the chemicals.

11:17 p.m. A man complained that his neighbor in the 3300 block of Après Ski Way kept playing the same song repeatedly at a very loud volume. He said he was willing to sign a complaint and wanted police to take the man to jail.

March 2

8:17 p.m. A man ordered a beer at a restaurant in the 700 block of Lincoln Avenue. When asked for identification, the man handed the server an underage ID. The man then realized he had handed the server his real ID when he had meant to show a fake ID, and he ran out of the restaurant. A report was taken.

. . . .

March 3

7:47 p.m. An employee of a grocery store in the 1800 block of Central Park Drive was given a ticket for throwing out more than $80 worth of food that should not have been thrown out. The employee said he knew he should not be throwing out the food and was mad at his supervisor.

. . . .

March 8

8:36 a.m. A man complained about a sock and a bottle of whiskey that were found in his yard in the 1500 block of Meadow Lane.

. . . .

March 11

11:37 p.m. A vehicle reportedly was toilet-papered in the 1100 block of Longview Circle.

. . . .

March 20

7:11 a.m. An injured skunk was reported running through the parking lot at Ace at the Curve. The skunk couldn't be located.

. . . .

March 25

7:36 a.m. A woman in the 2900 block of Abbey Road reportedly wanted police to pick up a dog that she no longer wanted. Officers explained that she would have to take the dog to the Steamboat Springs Animal Shelter, where it possibly would be euthanized. She decided to keep the dog.

April 7

5:56 a.m. A man reportedly was banging on a door in Mountain Village Circle. Officers gave him a courtesy transport to the Village Inn. All he wanted was breakfast.

. . . .

April 13

1:48 a.m. A 21-year-old man rolled his vehicle on Routt County Road 33 just past the James Brown Soul Center of the Universe Bridge. He then got out of the wreckage and walked to the Routt County Sheriff's Office to report his vehicle stolen. Splattered mud, blood and pieces of glass on the man led law enforcement officials to think otherwise.

. . . .

April 25

12:54 p.m. A woman reported that her neighbor, who was drunk, had come to her house while she was sleeping, woke her up and was talking to her. The man also had a stranger with him, the woman said.

. . . .

April 26

5:40 p.m. A report was made of a reckless driver in a Dodge pickup heading into town. The driver had crossed the double-yellow line six times and swerved off the road twice. The police contacted the driver and determined he was sober but had been eating while driving.

. . . .

April 27

9:17 p.m. A woman in the 600 block of Tamarack Drive reported her vehicle stolen. She later discovered that the vehicle had rolled down a nearby embankment. The car stopped in a ditch.

11:50 p.m. The owner of the tow truck that pulled the woman's car out of the ditch reported that his own vehicle rolled down an embankment at his home in the 3300 block of Après Ski Way. The truck sustained extensive damage.

April 29

11:09 p.m. Juveniles were cited for underage drinking near the Stock Bridge. A parent who came to pick up the juveniles was arrested on suspicion of driving under the influence of alcohol.

• • • • • • • • • • • • • • • •

May 1

4:25 p.m. Two young girls reported that three or four teenage boys drove by them as they were walking in the 400 block of Third Street, almost ran them off the road and asked whether they wanted candy.

• • • • • • • • • • • • • • • •

May 4

2:28 a.m. Police contacted an intoxicated man, who was barefoot, covered in mud and in the river near the 700 block of South Lincoln Avenue. After the police talked to the man, they deduced he had stolen a bike found earlier in the day. The man confessed and was arrested on suspicion of theft and being a minor in possession of alcohol.

• • • • • • • • • • • • • • • •

May 10

8:14 a.m. Residents called to complain about mattresses and couches that were left in their neighbor's yard in the 2500 block of Val D'Isere Drive. The neighbors said they had a yard sale and no one purchased the items, so they left them out hoping that people would take them. If the items are not gone by the weekend, the neighbors said they would put them away.

May 15

12:12 p.m. A complaint was made that two juveniles were riding on the roof of a car on Longview Circle. When the car would slam on the brakes, the juveniles would slide onto the hood.

• • • • • • • • • • • • • • • •

May 20

12:46 p.m. An officer was requested in the 1300 block of Mira Vista Court. The reporting party complained that a neighbor was going through her trash. She said the neighbor had done this before, but she was particularly concerned in this instance because the trash contained 10 years' worth of shredded W-2 forms.

• • • • • • • • • • • • • • • •

May 29

11:35 p.m. A 19-year-old woman in the Mountain Village Circle reported that a 50-year-old man with alcohol knocked on her door and wanted to know if the woman wanted to party.

• • • • • • • • • • • • • • • •

June 2

11:33 p.m. Three children were reported stealing a stop sign in the area of Village Drive and Après Ski Way. The sign was stolen, and the children could not be found.

• • • • • • • • • • • • • • • •

June 3

7:31 p.m. Children reportedly were throwing gummy bears at car windows in the 800 block of Lincoln Avenue and were warned.

• • • • • • • • • • • • • • • •

June 4

12:52 p.m. A stolen vehicle was reported in the 1900 block of Ski Time Square Drive. Police discovered that the vehicle had not been stolen. The driver, who had been drunk the night before, could not remember where he parked it.

June 5

7:05 p.m. Boys were reported sitting on the roof of Soda Creek Elementary School. The boys then jumped off the roof and left on bikes. The boys were contacted later and warned not to sit on the roof.

• • • • • • • • • • • • • • • •

June 7

3:44 p.m. A person being pulled on a skateboard by a tractor was reported on Fourth Street, but officers were unable to locate the person.

11:32 p.m. Several suspicious phone calls were reported at a residence on Pine Street. A person called a residence and said he or she was hurt, then called back and said he or she wanted to chat and then started talking about a guinea pig.

• • • • • • • • • • • • • • • •

June 8

12:48 p.m. A wounded and bleeding chipmunk was reported in a gutter in the 500 block of Lincoln Avenue. Police were unable to locate the animal.

• • • • • • • • • • • • • • • •

June 9

3:03 p.m. Children reportedly were throwing water balloons at vehicles in the 500 block of Tamarack Drive. They were warned by police.

4:24 p.m. A skunk stuck in a trap was reported in the area of Uncochief Circle.

• • • • • • • • • • • • • • • •

June 11

1:16 a.m. Officers were called when a woman from out of town let her children go fishing and then couldn't find them. They were later found fishing at Casey's Pond.

June 12

4:34 a.m. Two teenagers reportedly were riding their bikes and acting "really weird" in a parking lot in the 2300 block of Après Ski Way. Police checked out the situation and found nothing was wrong.

• • • • • • • • • • • • • • • •

June 13

12:42 a.m. Two possible burglars were reported climbing through the drive-through window at a business in the 200 block of Anglers Drive. It turned out to be two employees who had been locked out. Their employer let them in after they attempted to get into the business through the window. The employees reportedly quit after retrieving their personal items.

• • • • • • • • • • • • • • • •

June 15

11:47 a.m. A homeless man was reported singing and dancing in front of a business in the 700 block of Lincoln Avenue. Officers contacted him and told him to move along.

• • • • • • • • • • • • • • • •

June 20

2:21 a.m. A drunken man reported being assaulted in the 1800 block of Ski Time Square Drive. He later told police he might not have been assaulted. Officers advised him to come to the police station when he wasn't drunk to file a report.

May 12

1:05 a.m. A 19-year-old man in Dream Island was taken to the hospital after shooting his pinky finger with a rifle. The man was cleaning the rifle when it accidentally discharged.

June 23

8:22 a.m. A man reportedly was dumping cat excrement in the trash can of a government office in the 200 block of Lincoln Avenue. The man reportedly has been dumping cat excrement in the can for years. Officers were unable to locate the man.

• • • • • • • • • • • • • • • •

June 25

8:42 p.m. A person standing outside in the 1800 block of Central Park Drive reportedly saw a baggie blowing by with weeds in it. She reported the incident and gave the baggie to police. It did not contain enough material in it to test whether it was an illegal substance.

• • • • • • • • • • • • • • • •

June 27

11:24 a.m. A baby bird reportedly was stuck between a window and a display case in the 700 block of Lincoln Avenue.

• • • • • • • • • • • • • • • •

June 30

1:39 p.m. A mother requested that officers go with her to take a young boy to a business in the 200 block of Caribou Lane to return several rocks he had stolen earlier in the day. The boy's mother wanted police to help her teach her son that stealing is wrong.

• • • • • • • • • • • • • • • •

July 3

9:44 p.m. A fireworks complaint was reported on Short Street. Officers notified Routt County Communications that they would not be taking any more fireworks complaints because of the lack of officer manpower and the sheer volume of fireworks calls.

July 31

10:55 p.m. A bear reportedly was eating dog food in the mudroom of a home in the 200 block of Locust Court. The people home at the time were on the second floor, but they heard the bear snorting and making noises. The bear was gone when police arrived.

July 3

4:51 p.m. Officers were called to the baseball fields in the 2500 block of Pine Grove Road after 15 to 20 fans were reported fighting. After one woman punched another woman in the face, she received a citation for assault. Triple Crown officials were called to calm the crowd after officers threatened to close the fields if the fighting continued. Several fans were asked to leave the baseball fields as a result.

• • • • • • • • • • • • • • • •

July 4

10:42 p.m. A 19-year-old man involved in a fight reportedly led police on a short foot chase near Howelsen Hill. He was found in a trash Dumpster and arrested on charges of disorderly conduct and minor in possession of alcohol.

• • • • • • • • • • • • • • • •

July 8

1:37 a.m. Seven harassing phone calls were reported in the first block of Logan Avenue. The calls reportedly began at midnight and consisted of "heavy breathing."

July 9

1:25 p.m. Police were called to Emerald Park after a parent became unruly and began yelling at a referee during a sporting event. The parent was asked to leave, and the referee followed him out of the sporting area. Police arrived on scene to help calm the situation.

• • • • • • • • • • • • • • • •

July 12

5:40 p.m. An elderly woman reported her smoke alarm beeping because of a low battery in the 1800 block of Bear Drive, she was unable to change it, so firefighters responded and changed the battery for her.

• • • • • • • • • • • • • • • •

July 17

1:16 a.m. A person reportedly noticed that a small hole had been cut in the wall between the men's bathroom and a stall in the women's bathroom at a business in the 500 block of Lincoln Avenue. Managers were notified.

• • • • • • • • • • • • • • • •

July 20

12:29 p.m. Someone reportedly was shooting paintballs at gondola cars in the 2300 block of Après Ski Way, but officers were unable to locate the person.

3:37 p.m. A man in the 600 block of Spring Hill Road requested officers inspect cargo he was transporting in a van for a national Boy Scout Jamboree. The man said the van had to be inspected and cleared by police in order to enter the event. Officers confirmed that the contents of the van were safe and secured it with tags.

July 22

1:20 p.m. Several people reportedly were harassing a bear in the 1500 block of Kinnikinnick. The people were trying to scare the bear away by throwing rocks at it and yelling because it was eating trash.

• • • • • • • • • • • • • • • •

July 24

8:08 a.m. A magpie reportedly was flying in a store in the 1400 block of Lincoln Avenue.

• • • • • • • • • • • • • • • •

July 25

7:21 p.m. Two boys reportedly were playing baseball in the 3300 block of Meadow Lane. After one of their baseballs hit a neighbor's window and almost broke it, the neighbor reportedly took the children's baseball, and they continued to play with rocks. The boys had gone home when officers arrived.

• • • • • • • • • • • • • • • •

July 27

12:00 a.m. A woman reported hearing people splashing in her pond in the 2900 block of Honeysuckle Lane, but it turned out to be a bear, and officers scared it off.

• • • • • • • • • • • • • • • •

Aug. 1

10:46 a.m. A porta-potty allegedly was set on fire in the 800 block of Howelsen Parkway. Moderate damage was reported.

11:54 p.m. Loud noise was reported in the 1500 block of Shadow Run Court. When officers arrived, they found the residents playing strip poker, and they were warned for being loud.

Aug. 27

3:55 p.m. Someone reported that a man was washing his hands at the water treatment plant. When an officer went to investigate, he found the man was just panning for gold.

9:01 p.m. A fire reportedly was started in a portable bathroom in the 800 block of Howelsen Parkway. The fire was extinguished before officers arrived. There was damage and the incident is under investigation. The same bathroom had been lit on fire before.

Oct. 3

Aug. 2

3:15 p.m. A woman reported her car being keyed in the 100 block of Lincoln Avenue and found a note on her windshield saying that if she ever parked like that again, she would be buying a new windshield and tires. A report was taken.

. . . .

Aug. 8

12:48 p.m. An elderly man in an inner tube was stuck in the Yampa River near Rotary Park. The current pushed him into the willows on the bank of the river. He got frustrated and sat on a rock until someone could help him.

. . . .

Aug. 18

1:11 a.m. A drunken man reportedly was walking down the hallway of a hotel in the 3200 block of Lincoln Avenue and buying a soda from the vending machine. The man reportedly did the same thing last week and was warned by employees that the hotel "was not a 7-Eleven." Officers took a report.

. . . .

Aug. 22

2:25 p.m. A kitten reportedly was rescued from a car engine in the 1800 block of Central Park Drive.

Aug. 31

10:07 p.m. Emotions reportedly were "running high" in the 200 block of Howelsen Parkway. Officers walked through the area, and everything was fine.

. . . .

Sept. 8

3:27 p.m. A hairless fox was reportedly seen on Whistler Road. The animal was gone when officers arrived.

. . . .

Sept. 12

6:33 p.m. A man was reportedly trying to sell a freezer full of meat from the back of his truck in the 100 block of Hillside Drive. The vehicle was gone when officers arrived.

. . . .

Sept. 14

10:55 a.m. A man reportedly was calling local massage therapists and requesting lewd favors. Officers contacted the man and warned him.

. . . .

Sept. 22

5:14 p.m. A pair of nunchucks were found in the 1700 block of Meadow Lane.

. . . .

Sept. 23

11:01 a.m. A business in the 1100 block of Lincoln Avenue reportedly received a few unusual calls. A man called saying he was a Green Beret and complained about hiring procedures. A woman called complaining about charges made to her credit card, and a man called asking the employee to take her shirt off.

. . . .

Sept. 30

9:02 p.m. A woman reportedly fell off a barstool in the first block of Eighth Street and hit her head on the way down. The woman reportedly only had one martini. She was taken to the hospital by ambulance.

Sept. 30

11:57 p.m. A magnitude 4.1 earthquake was reported in Steamboat Springs. No damage or injuries were reported.

• • • • • • • • • • • • • • •

Oct. 10

7:49 p.m. Security officers in the 1800 block of Central Park Drive reportedly thought a man had stolen food even though the grocery store is closed for remodeling. The man left a note saying he would pay for the food later.

• • • • • • • • • • • • • • •

Oct. 14

11:13 p.m. A man reportedly tried to steal candy and Top Ramen soup from the 1800 block of Central Park Drive. Officers caught the man, and when he tried to run from them, he ran into the sliding glass door of the store. He was arrested on suspicion of theft.

• • • • • • • • • • • • • • •

Oct. 15

8:39 a.m. A woman on Columbine Drive reported being woken up the night before by arguing voices and two gunshots. She told police she was very tired at the time and might have dreamed the noise.

• • • • • • • • • • • • • • •

Oct. 17

5:27 p.m. A man reportedly was shooting his new gun in the 28000 block Yellow Jacket Drive. The man's neighbor confronted him about the gunfire, and although they had a pleasant conversation, the neighbor's wife became concerned when her husband hadn't returned. When the man who was shooting the gun showed up to apologize to his neighbor's wife, the wife called police officers thinking something had happened to her husband. Officers found that the man had gone to do some work after his conversation with the neighbor.

Aug. 29

5:11 p.m. Two juveniles reportedly were hitchhiking on U.S. Highway 40 and holding signs that read, "Going to Denver, we support marijuana." The boys were contacted and advised.

Oct. 25

3:30 p.m. A "mean little kitty" reportedly was stuck on a roof in the 2600 block of Riverside Drive.

• • • • • • • • • • • • • • •

Nov. 3

11:31 a.m. Two "vicious" dogs reportedly would not let a FedEx delivery man out of his truck to deliver a package in the 1400 block of Conestoga Circle.

• • • • • • • • • • • • • • •

Nov. 10

7:34 p.m. Construction workers reportedly were jackhammering and pounding away in the 2500 block of Village Drive. The workers were given a verbal warning and quit working.

• • • • • • • • • • • • • • •

Nov. 15

9:56 a.m. A woman on Maple Street reported that her 19-year-old son had used her credit card to accrue a $1,000 bill from calling 900-numbers instead of using it for groceries.

11:53 p.m. A man in the 400 block of Ore House Plaza reported that his neighbor was plugging an extension cord into his outside outlet to steal his electricity. The man was concerned that his neighbor was on drugs and was acting out against him.

Dec. 15

Nov. 17

3:11 p.m. A man in the 800 block of Anglers Drive became irate at the Department of Motor Vehicle licensing office when an employee told him he would have to wait his turn in line for service. The man was told to leave the office.

. . . .

Nov. 21

2:24 p.m. Skateboarders riding down Walton Creek Road reportedly were using the police department's Smart Trailer, which clocks drivers' speeds, to clock how fast they were going.

. . . .

Nov. 28

9:10 a.m. A man saying he was "Andre from Romania" was asking people for money in the 800 block of Douglas Street. Officers told him to ask for money elsewhere.

. . . .

Dec. 2

10:19 p.m. People on Montview Court reportedly were snowboarding down a homemade ramp and were making too much noise. Officers gave the residents a verbal warning.

. . . .

Dec. 6

12:00 p.m. A large, white dog in the 1400 block of Bob Adams Drive reportedly was tied up and barking all day "annoying the heck out of everybody." The dog was taken to the shelter.

Dec. 7

4:54 p.m. A snow-removal machine in the 400 block of Lincoln Avenue reportedly hit a lamp pole. The plow knocked the pole over, and the pole landed on a car. A report was taken.

. . . .

Dec. 14

8:45 a.m. A woman in the 3000 block of Village Drive reported finding pornographic photos stuffed in a dryer with her underwear.

. . . .

Dec. 19

8:18 p.m. A person in the 2100 block of Downhill Drive reported seeing a white SUV tying a strap to a stop sign and trying to pull the sign out of the ground. The stop sign was still there, and the car was gone when officers arrived.

2006

Aug. 1

4:33 p.m. A woman reported another woman walking a cat that was on a harness. The cat looked sick, and the caller was concerned about its welfare.

Jan. 1

1:23 p.m. Police responded to a report from the Gondola Square security office that a man was using someone else's ski pass. Police discovered the man had cut the ski pass off a 12-year-old girl.

5:26 p.m. A possible flasher was reported at the Sinclair station on U.S. Highway 40.

. . . .

Jan. 5

3:07 p.m. A woman in the 800 block of Lincoln Avenue reported that her 3-year-old child had locked her out of her car. Officers helped the woman get back into the car.

. . . .

Jan. 10

9:20 p.m. A man on Blue Sage Drive called police to complain about several illegally parked cars on the street and became angry because he said the officers would do nothing about it. The man said that he wanted to file a complaint against the police department and that he "was doing his research."

. . . .

Jan. 11

12:11 p.m. A woman in the 3300 block of Après Ski Way reportedly came home and found a drunken man sleeping on her couch. The man left when she asked him to.

. . . .

Jan. 12

12:23 p.m. Two Shi Tzu dogs locked in a car at a hotel parking lot reportedly were standing on the car's steering wheel and honking the horn. Officers left a warning notice on the car window for the owner.

. . . .

Jan. 18

3:16 a.m. A man shoveling his driveway in the 2500 block of Val D'Isere Circle reported two growling Rottweilers running at him. Officers were not able to find the dogs.

Jan. 17 7:32 p.m. Three men wearing only underwear and baseball caps reportedly ran through a restaurant in the 700 block of Lincoln Avenue. The men ran through the back door of the establishment. Officers were unable to find them.

Jan. 26

11:09 a.m. A woman in the 30000 block of Routt County Road 37 in Hayden called police because she thought something exploded in her pantry. The woman apparently was reaching for a bag of dog food on the top shelf of her pantry and accidentally tipped over a bottle of pepper spray. The bottle's trigger was depressed and sprayed noxious fumes into the woman's kitchen. The woman inhaled some of the fumes but refused to be taken to the hospital. Emergency crews did not need to fumigate the home or do anything other than let the spray settle.

. . . .

Jan. 31

4:05 p.m. Someone on Village Drive called to report a driver talking on his cellphone.

10:25 p.m. A woman in the 3000 block of Village Drive reported hearing loud music and seeing people urinating in the bushes and stealing bicycles. Officers contacted the individuals and told them to turn down the music and to stop stealing bicycles and urinating in bushes.

Feb. 6

2:52 p.m. A man reported losing a clipboard with his credit card and driver's license at the police department.

. . . .

Feb. 7

12:33 p.m. A woman in the 800 block of Lincoln Avenue reported her male roommate harassing her after she told him she was not interested in him. The woman told police her roommate began harassing her about trivial things such as how the other roommates did their laundry after she turned down the man's advances. A report was taken.

. . . .

Feb. 13

1:43 p.m. A dog reportedly was chasing skiers and snowmobilers on Headwall ski run. The dog was taken to the animal shelter.

. . . .

Feb. 17

3:06 p.m. A woman in the 300 block of Kelhi Court reported someone turning on her outside water faucet and letting the water run all night. A report was taken.

. . . .

Feb. 20

12:22 p.m. A woman in the 800 block of Grand Street reported two young men trespassing on her property and crouching behind shrubs to scare the elk. Officers contacted the two men and wrote them tickets for trespassing and disturbing wildlife.

. . . .

Feb. 22

10:19 a.m. A woman in the 500 block of Parkview Drive reported receiving harassing phone calls from another woman. The woman receiving the calls told police she was having an affair with a married man and suspected that the woman who was calling her was his wife. A report was taken.

March 1

12:06 p.m. A hotel employee in the 2200 block of Village Inn Court reportedly found a bag of marijuana and a marijuana pipe while he was cleaning a room and called hotel security. When officers arrived, the person staying in the room had returned, and he told officers the marijuana and pipe were his friend's and that his friend must have left it in his room. During a later interview, after police asked the man why he didn't call police when he found his friend's belongings, the man shrugged and told the officers the drugs were his. He was given a citation.

. . . .

March 13

10:56 p.m. A woman in the 1300 block of Walton Creek Road reported that her loud, college-age neighbors were "about to come through the walls." The woman told police her noisy neighbors were an ongoing problem. The residents were contacted and told to quiet down.

. . . .

March 15

1:21 p.m. A 70-year-old woman reportedly stuffed a shirt from a business in the 600 block of Lincoln Avenue into her purse and left the store without paying. An 8-month pregnant clerk saw the woman and confronted her outside the store. The elderly woman told the clerk she didn't steal anything and began to walk away. The pregnant woman reached into the woman's purse, grabbed the shirt and ran after her as she attempted to get away. The elderly woman got into her car and drove off. The pregnant clerk called police and gave them the woman's license plate number. Officers later contacted the woman and gave her a citation for theft.

March 16

5:01 p.m. A man in the 2000 block of Storm Meadows Drive reported seeing several snowboarders preparing to jump off a fourth-story balcony onto a ski slope. Officers told the snowboarders not to jump.

. . . .

March 20

9:57 p.m. A woman in the 2300 block of Mount Werner Road reported her son missing after the family returned from a sleigh ride. Apparently, the child had fallen asleep in the back of the bus the family was riding in, and the bus driver left before the family realized the child was on the bus. Officers contacted the bus driver, woke the child up and returned him to his family.

. . . .

March 22

12:35 p.m. A woman in the 100 block of Sequoia Court thought someone broke into her house because the front door was ajar. Officers later found that the woman's Realtor couldn't get into the home because the door was stuck and accidentally splintered the door when she shoved it open.

March 23

2:24 p.m. Someone in the 2700 block of Laurel Lane reportedly saw two people having sex in the back of a white Ford Explorer. An officer contacted the couple and told them their behavior was inappropriate for a city street.

. . . .

April 4

1:07 a.m. A Steamboat Springs Transit employee reported a man in his 20s standing under a bus shelter but not responding to the employee's voice. The employee told police the man was drooling and might be intoxicated.

. . . .

April 7

10:37 p.m. A woman near Strawberry Park Elementary School told several juveniles who were riding snowboards on school property to go home. The juveniles then began throwing snowballs at the woman. Officers contacted the snowboarders and gave them a warning.

. . . .

April 10

2:01 p.m. A man reportedly was attacked by a brown and tan snake on a bike trail in the 2700 block of Village Drive. The man told officers the snake attacked him and two dogs. When officers arrived, the snake had disappeared under a snowbank.

March 7

8:23 a.m. A 17-year-old Steamboat Springs boy was arrested in the high school parking lot on suspicion of stealing something from a car. Officers reportedly hid under a blanket in the car the boy was stealing from and baited him with money left in the car's cupholder. When the boy opened the car door, the officer jumped up and caught him. The boy was compliant with officers and even opened the back door of the car for the officer to get out. He was charged with several counts of felony trespassing and theft.

> **11:18 p.m.** A neighbor reported a car being wrapped in Saran Wrap on Mountain Village Circle. There was no damage to the car, and the officer said it looked like a "Ford deli sandwich."
>
> *April 8*

April 26
8:32 p.m. A drunken man reportedly tried to take a to-go order from Chelsea's Restaurant in Oak Creek without paying for it. The restaurant's bartender chased the man and took the food. Officers said they contacted the man and told him to pay for the food or they would file charges against him.

April 27
10:03 p.m. A woman in the 3100 block of Ingles Lane reported a raccoon on her lawn, spinning in circles, foaming at the mouth and vomiting. The woman was concerned the animal had rabies. Officers put the animal down.

April 29
9:42 p.m. Police received a report of a basset hound that had crashed a wedding reception being held at the Steamboat Springs Community Center. Police took the uninvited dog to the animal shelter.

May 5
2:04 a.m. A woman reported "a herd of bears" outside her home in the 200 block of Hillside Drive. The bears were gone when officers arrived.

May 7
1:15 p.m. A drunken man in the 44000 block of Routt County Road 36 reported someone eating a package of barbecue ribs that were sent to him several weeks ago. Officers contacted the man's coworkers, who told police they ate the ribs because they were sent to the man's place of employment for a party. A report was taken.

May 11
10:22 a.m. A woman called police and reported that a man was taking mulch that did not belong to him in the 200 block of Howelsen Parkway. Police advised the man that the mulch was not free.

May 14
11:22 a.m. A woman reported wildlife in the 1400 block of Clubhouse Drive. Police said a bear broke into a Ford Explorer that had food items inside. Police said the bear broke in through the rear passenger window, damaged the leather seats and "tore the heck out of the inside of the car."

May 17
2:13 p.m. Officers issued warnings to about 40 people who were playing paintball at a park on Anglers Drive.

8:43 p.m. A man in the 600 block of Mountain Village Circle reported his neighbor stomping on the floor and "having something hard in the dryer."

May 18
2:48 p.m. Officers spoke to someone in the 300 block of Seventh Street about "why it's bad to steal."

> **1:50 p.m.** A woman reported seeing a dog running near Fifth and Yampa streets with a wooden chair attached to its leash. The dog was gone when officers arrived.
>
> **May 15**

May 25

9:28 p.m. A 29-year-old woman in the 2400 block of Lincoln Avenue was arrested on suspicion of harassment after she hit her soon-to-be ex-husband three or four times on the arm with a paint can. Police said the couple was arguing about how loud the woman was playing on the computer, which was interfering with the man watching a movie. After the man tried to shut the woman's door, the woman turned up the computer's volume and hit the man with the paint can.

9:38 p.m. Security officers in the 1800 block of Ski Time Square reported three young men jumping from rooftop to rooftop shooting at one another and holding guns. Officers contacted the men, who were shooting soft pellet guns, and told them to leave the area.

· · · · · · · · · · · · · · · ·

May 26

12:28 a.m. A man reported a wad of paper on fire in the 700 block of Lincoln Avenue. Someone stepped on it and put out the fire.

8:21 a.m. A man and woman reportedly thought a bear was trying to break into their house in the 1100 block of Blue Sage Drive. The bear reportedly stood on top of the couple's hot tub to get at a bird feeder full of food. An officer scared the bear away.

June 2

6:20 p.m. Someone reportedly stole some old barbed wire from a fence in the 100 block of Logan Street.

· · · · · · · · · · · · · · · ·

June 6

4:16 a.m. A drunken man in the 2300 block of Mount Werner Circle claimed to have lost his monkey. Police said they were trying to help the man find his way home and turned him over to his father. The man's father told police that his son does have a monkey and they would find it in the morning.

· · · · · · · · · · · · · · · ·

June 22

1:21 a.m. A man went to the police department to tell officers that the federal government owed him money.

8:49 a.m. A man reported seeing another man "taking a bath" in the 3400 block of Airport Circle. Officers contacted the man and were told he was just changing his shirt, not bathing.

· · · · · · · · · · · · · · · ·

June 26

8:10 a.m. A woman reported seeing a "group of hippies" camping on the grass next to the Mount Werner Road off-ramp on U.S. Highway 40. Officers gave the campers a warning.

· · · · · · · · · · · · · · · ·

June 27

4:12 p.m. A man on Routt County Road 129 reportedly hit his neighbor's cow with an all-terrain vehicle because he was upset the cow was on his property. Officers gave a warning to the man. The cow was not injured.

· · · · · · · · · · · · · · · ·

Aug. 2

10:45 p.m. A man reportedly was smoking marijuana by a motel in the 300 block of South Lincoln Avenue. Officers located the man and discovered he was smoking blades of grass, not marijuana.

Aug. 5

12:01 a.m. A nude man was reported walking around the parking lot of Fish Creek Falls Condos. When officers approached the man in his apartment, he was wearing jeans, a miniskirt and a buttondown shirt. They found pornographic material in his condo. He was arrested on probable cause for indecent exposure.

. . . .

Aug. 8

7:49 p.m. A badger reportedly wandered into a store in the 700 block of Lincoln Avenue and was chased into a Chinese restaurant by an employee. Colorado Division of Wildlife officers handled the loose badger.

. . . .

Aug. 15

5:40 p.m. A man reportedly was "on his break" and "smoking stuff out of a pipe that wasn't tobacco" in the 1800 block of Kamar Plaza.

. . . .

Aug. 16

1:21 p.m. A young man was shaking his fists and making obscene gestures at a driver in the 400 block of Blue Sage Circle.

. . . .

Aug. 28

4:57 p.m. Three people reportedly "were sitting on the grass smoking pot" in the 700 block of Lincoln Avenue.

. . . .

Aug. 30

2:51 p.m. A bronzed bird's nest affixed to a rock in front of a statue of a family reportedly was stolen from The Sanctuary near Redwood Drive. Police said the nest, which is worth about $5,000, had been stolen off the rock several times.

Sept. 6

12:36 p.m. A property owner in the 1000 block of Uncochief Circle was upset that someone put a trampoline on her vacant lot. Officers mediated the situation and had the trampoline moved.

. . . .

Sept. 7

4:58 p.m. A woman at the police department had questions about why a police car had been parked in front of her house two nights in a row.

. . . .

Sept. 10

12:47 a.m. An employee at a bar in the 1800 block of Ski Time Square Drive reported a patron was causing a disturbance. A man had a broken broom handle up his sleeve. He told police he had it because some people attempted to jump him earlier that night.

. . . .

Sept. 12

6:57 p.m. Two dogs reportedly were pulling a man on a bike down the middle of Tamarack and Lupine drives. The dogs and bicyclist were gone when officers arrived.

June 13

5:34 p.m. A bear reportedly broke through a screen door in the 500 block of Steamboat Boulevard and broke into a pantry. The residents found the bear sitting on its haunches eating peanut butter. The bear was gone when officers arrived.

Sept. 16

3:53 p.m. An officer was summoned to the 2000 block of Golf Course Road after snowboarders reportedly brought snow into town and were riding rails.

· · · · · · · · · · · · · · · ·

Sept. 18

5:49 p.m. A man stole a grocery cart from a store in the 1400 block of Lincoln Avenue. The man began to run with the cart after he realized he was being chased.

· · · · · · · · · · · · · · · ·

Sept. 19

3:41 a.m. Two or three intoxicated college students reportedly called a Steamboat Springs police officer's personal cellphone and yelled obscenities at him when he answered it. The officer was able to find where the men lived and contacted them at their home in the 1000 block of The Boulevard. A 20-year-old Steamboat Springs man at the home was arrested on suspicion of being a fugitive of justice, and police confiscated two glass pipes used for smoking marijuana.

Oct. 1

4:01 p.m. A person reported a boy in a black trench coat was wielding a machete near the intersection of Seventh and Oak streets. Police contacted the boy at the Indian Trails bus stop. The boy told police he had purchased the blade online with his parent's permission and he was taking it to a friend's house to make a handle. Police took the boy home.

· · · · · · · · · · · · · · · ·

Oct. 2

8:13 a.m. A woman in the 40000 block of Lindsay Drive reportedly saw some "suspicious lights in the sky."

· · · · · · · · · · · · · · · ·

Oct. 5

7:55 p.m. A black bear reportedly stole a garbage can out of a garage in the 3000 block of Trails Edge. Officers scared off the bear.

· · · · · · · · · · · · · · · ·

Oct. 9

9:33 p.m. A woman in the 300 block of Pearl Street was concerned that her dog was constantly barking at something in the lawn. Officers did not find anything in the woman's lawn.

· · · · · · · · · · · · · · · ·

Oct. 11

12:33 a.m. A 21-year-old Steamboat Springs man was arrested near Village Drive and Walton Creek Road on suspicion of theft and failing to appear in court. Police said the man may have stolen some construction cones and a "giant electrical generator" and put them in the middle of the road.

· · · · · · · · · · · · · · · ·

Oct. 24

2:06 p.m. A woman reportedly sat in a restaurant's parking lot in her car all day in the 200 block of Lincoln Avenue.

Oct. 27

10:42 p.m. A woman in the 1400 block of Pine Grove Road reported a loud band playing at a restaurant. Police said "there was nothing to do about that."

. . . .

Oct. 30

5:33 a.m. Someone driving in the 900 block of Lincoln Avenue reported being flagged down by a man wearing nothing but a black fleece jacket and boxers. A report was taken.

. . . .

Nov. 2

9:06 p.m. A 19-year-old Steamboat Springs man reportedly was standing naked, yelling in a parking lot in the 1800 block of Central Park Drive. The man was under the influence of drugs and not cooperative when he was contacted by officers. He was restrained and taken to the hospital for treatment. The man later was taken to jail on an outstanding warrant.

. . . .

Nov. 5

4:46 p.m. A woman called police to report another woman who appeared to be intoxicated and was pushing a baby stroller near Seventh and Aspen streets. Police contacted the woman, who was intoxicated, but there was no baby in the stroller. The woman told police she did not know where her baby was. Police learned that the baby was at home with its father. Police contacted the Health and Human Services Department.

. . . .

Nov. 6

9:55 p.m. A man in Wisconsin reportedly called his wife during halftime of a football game and told her he would call back when the game was over. When the man called back, the woman did not answer the phone, and the man was concerned something had happened to her. Officers checked on the woman, and she was fine.

Nov. 8

12:20 p.m. A visiting businessman reportedly became enraged by a loud car radio while he was stopped at a stoplight near Hilltop Parkway and Lincoln Avenue. Police said the man was talking on his cellphone with his windows rolled up and couldn't hear his conversation. The man then pulled up next to the car with the loud radio and began shaking a water bottle at the car and squirting water in the car's open window. The driver of the car with the "loud radio" followed the man to his hotel and called police. Officers mediated the situation and gave both men warnings.

. . . .

Nov. 14

5:12 p.m. A 22-year-old Steamboat Springs man near Third Street and Lincoln Avenue was arrested on suspicion of driving under suspension, failing to notify police of an accident, leaving the scene of an accident and not having registration. The man reportedly struck a principal's car and left the scene of the accident. The principal followed the man, stopped him and told him he was a police officer and asked for the man's car keys. When police arrived, they warned the principal not to impersonate a law enforcement officer.

. . . .

Nov. 15

12:35 p.m. A Jehovah's Witness who was walking door to door in the 600 block of Anglers Drive reportedly came upon a house with a broken window that had fresh blood on the windowsill. Police said the blood belonged to a dog that had broken the window jumping out of the home. The dog was OK.

Nov. 19

4:04 p.m. A 50-year-old Steamboat Springs woman was arrested in the 3300 block of Covey Circle on suspicion of misdemeanor theft and felony second-degree burglary. Police said the woman was caught on tape breaking into her ex-boyfriend's home in the 3300 block of Meadow Lane and taking two bottles of wine and $100.

Nov. 21

10:34 a.m. A man in the 2100 block of Bear Drive was concerned when his dog brought home a piece of raw meat because he thought it had been poisoned. Animal control officers said there were no signs of foul play.

10:45 a.m. Two teenagers reportedly were asked to leave the 200 block of Anglers Drive because of their public display of affection, but they did not leave. Instead, the teens began smoking cigarettes in front of a business door. The teens were gone when officers arrived.

Nov. 22

5:48 p.m. A man went into the tattoo parlor in the 1400 block of Pine Grove Road and threatened a tattoo artist with a crow bar because he refused to give him a Hell's Angels tattoo.

Nov. 28

10:56 p.m. A man in the 3300 block of Après Ski Way was annoyed that his neighbor was using a loud leaf blower to clear snow from his driveway. Police told the man using the leaf blower to turn it off.

Dec. 7

7:02 p.m. A woman in the 3100 block of Lincoln Avenue was upset she received "attitude" from a group of young people she had asked to stop smoking.

Dec. 11

12:07 a.m. Five or six young people reportedly were swinging ski poles and trying to hit cars with them near Après Ski Way and Village Drive.

Dec. 12

3:49 p.m. Someone on Lincoln Avenue reportedly pulled up next to a man waiting at a bus stop and stared at him. A report was taken.

Dec. 18

9:26 a.m. A man was caught using a woman's ski pass at the Steamboat Ski Area.

Dec. 24

6:08 p.m. A dog escaped from his kennel at the animal shelter and set off a burglar alarm motion detector. Some missing dog biscuits are still under investigation.

Dec. 31

3:40 p.m. Vandalism was reported in Phippsburg. A sergeant with the Routt County Sheriff's Office said a resident pushed over his neighbor's fence because the resident did not like where the fence was.

· · · · · · · · 2007 · · · · · · · ·

Oct. 17

5:53 p.m. A woman was stuck in her car in the 1800 block of Christie Drive because a bear was "staring at her from the woods." The bear was gone when officers arrived.

Jan. 3

8:41 p.m. A 24-year-old Steamboat Springs man was arrested in the 1900 block of Ski Time Square Drive on suspicion of theft after he "stuffed a pair of women's mittens into his pockets." Police said the man allegedly stole the mittens from an all-women's clothing store and was then caught asking people for "scissors or something sharp" to cut the tags off the mittens. The man also had two outstanding warrants.

• • • • • • • • • • • • • • • •

Jan. 9

9:58 a.m. A shaggy dog wouldn't let a woman out of her house because it was sitting on her porch in the 800 block of Pine Street.

• • • • • • • • • • • • • • • •

Jan. 22

3:58 p.m. A 14-year-old girl came to the police department to ask a police officer to escort her home because she hadn't gone home the night before and "didn't want her dad to freak out." Officers mediated the situation.

• • • • • • • • • • • • • • • •

Jan. 23

10:07 a.m. A man in the 1900 block of Mount Werner Road couldn't find his car where he had parked it earlier in the week. Officers found the man's car across the street.

• • • • • • • • • • • • • • • •

Jan. 24

10:32 p.m. A Steamboat Springs police officer sat in on the Steamboat Springs City Council meeting to mediate a "potentially out-of-hand situation." No incidents were reported.

• • • • • • • • • • • • • • • •

Jan. 25

3:56 a.m. A man near Après Ski Way and Ski Trail Lane reportedly "felt bad" that he didn't stop for another man standing in the middle of the street wearing a sweatshirt and shorts jumping up and down trying to wave down cars. The man in the middle of the road was gone when officers arrived.

10:00 p.m. An intoxicated Colorado Mountain College student reportedly tried to run over his resident adviser in the 1300 block of Bob Adams Drive. Police said the RA was chasing the student before the student got in a car. The student then reportedly tried to drive over the RA before leaving the area. Police were unable to find the student.

March 1

Jan. 27

12:49 a.m. Police officers were called to the intersection of Village Drive and Walton Creek Road, where officers arrested a 30-year-old Steamboat Springs man on suspicion of misdemeanors including prohibited use of a weapon, possession of fireworks and throwing missiles at a vehicle. Police said the man was lighting bottle rockets and throwing them at cars "right in front of the police — go figure." No injuries or property damage resulted from the incident.

12:52 p.m. A juvenile situation was reported in Steamboat. Police said youths were allegedly "hood surfing," meaning one youth would sit or stand on the hood of a vehicle while another youth drove down the road, but police found no evidence of the reported incident after arriving at the scene.

Feb. 5

12:37 p.m. Ski patrol reportedly brought an intoxicated person down from the upper Mount Werner area. Police said the drunken man was "verbally obnoxious," and he was cited for disorderly conduct.

• • • • • • • • • • • • • • •

Feb. 9

11:33 p.m. A group of people reportedly were building snowboard jumps in the first block of Park Place. The group was gone when officers arrived.

• • • • • • • • • • • • • • •

Feb. 10

9:32 p.m. An 18-year-old Boulder man was arrested in the 1800 block of Ski Time Square on suspicion of indecent exposure, false reporting and being a minor in possession. Police said the man was wearing a thong and exposing himself to people as he was running down the streets.

• • • • • • • • • • • • • • •

Feb. 11

9:07 p.m. A police officer was requested at Gondola Transit Center near Steamboat Ski Area. Police said 10 men who appeared to be drunk were reportedly throwing snowballs at a bus and shouting obscenities. The suspects were gone when officers arrived.

Feb. 22

12:38 a.m. Officers warned people listening to "heavy bass music" in the 400 block of Tamarack Drive to turn it down.

• • • • • • • • • • • • • • •

Feb. 23

4:13 p.m. Children in the 700 block of Tamarack Drive reportedly were throwing apples and bananas at each other's doors and "made quite a mess." Police mediated the situation.

• • • • • • • • • • • • • • •

Feb. 25

2:37 p.m. Police warned young men who police said were "walking around with traffic cones on their heads" on 13th Street.

• • • • • • • • • • • • • • •

Feb. 26

2:06 p.m. Someone reportedly left a beauty salon in the 600 block of Marketplace Plaza without paying for his or her $41 haircut. A report was taken.

• • • • • • • • • • • • • • •

Feb. 27

6:41 p.m. A woman in the 100 block of Ninth Street reportedly found a "suspicious substance stuffed into an item" at her store. The woman suspected it was marijuana. Police seized the substance.

March 2

1:44 a.m. A baby girl was born in the chip aisle in the 7-Eleven at U.S. Highway 40 and Elk River Road. A Steamboat Springs police officer delivered the girl after her parents, who live in Craig, couldn't make it to the hospital in time.

March 1

8:13 a.m. A John Deere tractor reportedly was parked in the 100 block of Eighth Street, and someone was concerned that its hydraulic arm was going to come down and "kill someone." Officers warned the tractor's owner to move it.

· · · · · · · · · · · · · · · ·

March 6

5:32 a.m. Officers attempted to contact a woman at Curve Plaza who had been sleeping in her car. The woman drove off when officers approached her.

5:12 p.m. A woman near Skyview and Chinook lanes was concerned about a group of snowboarders and skiers using a jump to ski over an abandoned bus. A report was taken.

· · · · · · · · · · · · · · · ·

March 7

3:24 a.m. A group of juveniles reportedly were shooting off fireworks inside a home in the 3300 block of Après Ski Way. Officers gave the group a written warning.

March 7

9:16 p.m. A woman reported an incident involving a skit and a fake gun at a church in the 800 block of Dougherty Road. Police said the church's youth group put on a skit involving a fake gun, though none of the youths knew the gun was fake, and they hid under chairs after the actor put the gun to the youth director's head. Routt County Communications was aware of the skit and told the youth that the situation was under control when they began calling 911. Police mediated the situation.

· · · · · · · · · · · · · · · ·

March 9

3:35 a.m. A 22-year-old Steamboat Springs man was arrested in the 1800 block of Ski Time Square Drive on suspicion of driving under the influence of alcohol, first-degree motor vehicle theft, false reporting and failing to report an accident. Police said the man stole an Alpine Taxi while the taxi's driver was using a bathroom. Officers stopped the man near Steamboat Boulevard and Mount Werner Road after he reportedly ran into something.

March 23

3:53 p.m. A 34-year-old Steamboat Springs woman was arrested in the 800 block of Lincoln Avenue on suspicion of bribery, fraud and possessing a Schedule II controlled substance. Police said the woman called a pharmacy pretending to be a medical physician to get a prescription filled. When she went to the pharmacy, the woman reportedly was found possessing methamphetamine and tried to bribe a police officer with a winning lottery ticket to let her go. The woman was arrested and posted a $20,000 bond at the Routt County Jail.

March 12

9:31 p.m. A woman in the 900 block of Pine Street called police so her 8-year-old daughter could talk to them about her being a "terrible parent." Officers mediated the situation.

• • • • • • • • • • • • • • • •

March 15

11:24 p.m. A woman wanted to talk to an officer about "a date gone bad."

• • • • • • • • • • • • • • • •

March 17

8:57 a.m. A man reported vandalism in the 1800 block of Central Park Drive. Police said it appeared that somebody had set fire to a shopping cart, possibly using a chemical substance that melted part of the cart.

• • • • • • • • • • • • • • • •

March 23

9:17 a.m. A man came to the police department because he was "hearing voices" and suspected someone was investigating him and watching him. A report was taken.

• • • • • • • • • • • • • • • •

March 27

1:14 p.m. A man reported someone sleeping in a bus shelter near Shadow Run Frontage and Walton Creek Road. Officers woke the person up, and he said he was "just taking a nap."

• • • • • • • • • • • • • • • •

April 1

5:20 p.m. A 28-year-old Alabama man was arrested on suspicion of driving under the influence of alcohol and careless driving in Clark after he crashed the snowmobile he was driving in reverse down a muddy driveway. The man was not injured.

April 4

3:10 p.m. A group of renters in the 2000 block of Walton Creek Road destroyed the interior of the house by tearing drywall off the walls, discarding beer bottles and liquor bottles on the floors and spray-painting the walls with graffiti. Police estimated the damage around $20,000 to $30,000. The incident is under investigation.

11:01 p.m. A woman reportedly was sitting at a bar and "pulling her hair out" in the 3100 block of Lincoln Avenue. The person who called police thought the woman was on drugs. The woman was gone when officers arrived.

• • • • • • • • • • • • • • • •

April 12

12:30 a.m. A woman reported that her ex-boyfriend was harassing her by calling her "every 10 seconds."

• • • • • • • • • • • • • • • •

April 13

11:47 a.m. A woman in the 400 block of Dabney Lane reportedly was receiving threatening text messages in Spanish. The woman told police she needed a Spanish translator.

• • • • • • • • • • • • • • • •

April 18

9:56 a.m. A squealing pig reportedly was stuck between two barn doors in the 800 block of Howelsen Parkway. The pig was gone when animal control officers arrived.

April 21

8:44 p.m. A male threw a Frisbee to his off-leash dog on the corner of Tamarack and Buena Vista, and the dog ran in front of a police vehicle. The male was arrested on a warrant for a previous dog-at-large citation.

April 29

6:51 p.m. A couple reported seeing white smoke coming from a residence in the 3200 block of Snowflake Circle. Police said "someone's barbecue grill got away from them."

May 6

10:02 p.m. A bear reportedly was on the roof of a business in the 700 block of Lincoln Avenue. The bear jumped off the roof onto Lincoln Avenue and ran down Ninth Street before climbing a tree in Little Toots Park.

May 7

10:19 p.m. "Truckloads" of skateboarders reportedly were grinding in the 1300 block of Bob Adams Drive. Officers gave them a warning.

May 10

4:59 p.m. A man in the first block of Anglers Drive reported seeing two men in a car "roll a marijuana joint" and "break apart a marijuana bulb."

May 20

12:38 p.m. A woman reported an elderly woman driving down a bike path near the Fish Creek Mobile Home Park. Police were unable to locate the vehicle.

May 23

3:05 p.m. A man reported he hired somebody to do repairs on his townhome, and instead of doing repairs, the man reportedly started living at the townhome. The suspect also drank a lot of wine from the man's wine collection.

June 4

1:13 p.m. A man reportedly took a lawn mower that was sitting on the side of the road in the 900 block of Pine Street. The man told police he took the lawn mower because he thought it was free. The lawn mower was returned.

1:06 a.m. A man in his 20s reportedly was knocking on a door and yelling "hello" in the 200 block of Eighth Street. The man was gone when officers arrived.

June 13

11:35 a.m. A woman in the 1000 block of Central Park Drive reported being yelled at by an older woman about how loud her truck was. The woman was concerned the older woman was going to do something to her truck. A report was taken.

June 14
7:32 p.m. A "blonde, rough-looking" woman reportedly was saying "weird things" to another woman in the 800 block of Lincoln Avenue. The blonde woman also tried to pull the other woman's dog into her car. Police mediated the situation.

· · · · · · · · · · · · · · · ·

June 15
11:55 a.m. A postal worker reportedly found a sandwich bag of marijuana in a mailbox in the 400 block of Tamarack Drive. The incident is under investigation.

· · · · · · · · · · · · · · · ·

June 19
5:28 p.m. Several bicyclists reportedly were chasing a bear in the 1200 block of Lincoln Avenue.

June 4
8:17 a.m. Someone reportedly wrecked a donated golf cart used to escort people with disabilities around the Yampa River Botanic Park. Police said someone cut the cable to the golf cart, hot-wired it and drove it all over a soccer field, damaging several plastic pipes. The golf cart was found in a ditch near the railroad tracks. The incident is under investigation.

June 25
10:23 p.m. Juveniles were reported to be shooting water balloons at softball players in the 400 block of Howelsen Parkway. Police were unable to locate the juveniles.

· · · · · · · · · · · · · · · ·

June 28
8:07 a.m. A woman in the 2000 block of Lincoln Avenue reportedly saw an offensive poster of a woman holding a gun. Officers were unable to find any posters in the area.

· · · · · · · · · · · · · · · ·

July 2
4:31 p.m. A man in a baseball cap and "greasy T-shirt" reportedly scared a man and his two children by talking to them. Officers contacted the man and, everything was fine.

· · · · · · · · · · · · · · · ·

July 4
2:53 p.m. Officers warned four people in the 800 block of Howelsen Parkway not to jump off a bridge into the Yampa River.

· · · · · · · · · · · · · · · ·

July 11
4:32 p.m. Someone reportedly threw a cup of ice at a bicyclist near Lincoln Avenue and Hilltop Parkway. Officers contacted the people who threw the ice and gave them a warning.

· · · · · · · · · · · · · · · ·

July 15
4:54 p.m. A person complained about a horse chasing his 11-year-old son in the 100 block of Lincoln Avenue.

· · · · · · · · · · · · · · · ·

July 16
12:56 a.m. A man reportedly was "being creepy" in a wood-paneled van in the 700 block of Yampa Street. Officers took the drunken man to detox.

12:55 p.m. A bear broke into a home in the 2900 block of Ski Trail Lane. Police said the bear was sitting on a kitchen counter eating a bag of brown sugar. No injuries were reported, and the bear was scared out of the house. Several dishes and other items on the kitchen counter were damaged, police said.

Sept. 7

July 24

7:42 p.m. Juveniles throwing rocks with lacrosse sticks were reported in the 600 block of Lincoln Avenue. The juveniles were gone when police arrived.

. . . .

Aug. 3

4:02 p.m. An assault was reported in the 200 block of Howelsen Parkway. Police said a man punched another man in the face for running into his daughter on the Alpine slide at Howelsen Hill.

. . . .

Aug. 5

2:42 a.m. Gunshots were reported in the 43500 block of Routt County Road 36. The noise turned out to be from a nail gun someone was using to build a staircase.

. . . .

Aug. 9

9:38 a.m. A woman in the 10000 block of W. U.S. Highway 40 in Hayden reported finding several 6-inch red ribbons in her yard.

. . . .

Aug. 11

4:39 p.m. A juvenile reportedly called Domino's and ordered hundreds of dollars worth of food then called back to cancel the order.

. . . .

Aug. 13

9:09 a.m. An oxygen tank reportedly was rolling down the 900 block of Weiss Drive. A passerby picked up the tank before officers could arrive.

July 16

11:03 a.m. Someone reported that a "bad man" had passed out in his bed in the 400 block of Hilltop Parkway.

. . . .

July 17

6:32 p.m. Someone reported a woman selling tamales out of her car on Anchor Way.

. . . .

July 22

7:50 a.m. A man was found asleep in a running truck at Ninth Street and Lincoln Avenue. He was charged with DUI.

. . . .

July 23

9:51 a.m. A dead cat was found in the road in the 2500 block of Riverside Drive in Steamboat.

Aug. 21

10:22 a.m. A school's window was open in the 800 block of Oak Street, and ketchup had been spilled all over the floor. The incident is under investigation.

. . . .

Aug. 24

1:58 p.m. A man reportedly was interviewing women at a bar in the 3100 block of Lincoln Avenue "for modeling purposes." A report was taken.

. . . .

Aug. 27

2:17 a.m. A woman reportedly was yelling at a man who was throwing up. Police mediated the argument.

7:43 p.m. Three men reportedly were "mooning" cars near Pine Grove Road and Lincoln Avenue.

. . . .

Aug. 30

4:30 p.m. A woman in the 2600 block of Alpenglow Way complained about someone banging on bongo drums. The drummer was given a warning.

. . . .

Aug. 31

10:07 a.m. Someone reportedly found a urine sample in the 600 block of Marketplace Plaza.

. . . .

Sept. 12

3:34 a.m. A wild animal reportedly was in a woman's freezer in the 1800 block of Huckleberry Lane.

. . . .

Sept. 21

7:12 a.m. A man reported someone cutting sod away from his yard in the first block of Missouri Avenue. The man said there was a "dirt trail" leading away from the house.

Sept. 21

3:30 p.m. A woman in the 1000 block of 13th Street reportedly heard running water, found the lights on in the basement and an empty candy dish, and thought someone had broken in. Police said there was no sign of forced entry and no one else was around.

. . . .

Sept. 26

6:29 p.m. A woman in the 1800 block of Central Park Drive reported seeing a group of skaters wearing baggy pants, smoking and punching each other. The group was gone when officers arrived.

. . . .

Oct. 4

4:45 p.m. A woman in the 500 block of Evans Street thought she saw a man peeking through her windows. The woman locked herself in the bathroom with a can of pepper spray. Officers found the man who was at the woman's home to light the furnace.

. . . .

Oct. 23

12:27 p.m. A man in the 200 block of 12th Street found a chewed up elk leg at the end of his driveway.

Sept. 24

5:21 p.m. A man reported seeing a child dragging a cat around on a leash and throwing the cat in a puddle. Officers talked to the boy and his parents about the incident.

Oct. 25

2:26 a.m. A woman reported having an argument with her "couch-surfing" roommates in the 1300 block of Walton Creek Road. The roommates agreed to leave.

· · · · · · · · · · · · · · · ·

Nov. 16

8:38 p.m. A man complained that his wife took his children to a bar in Oak Creek.

· · · · · · · · · · · · · · · ·

Nov. 29

12:41 a.m. A group of snowboarders were reported to be riding rails near Park Avenue and Broad Street. They were contacted and asked to leave.

· · · · · · · · · · · · · · · ·

Dec. 4

9:16 a.m. An animal complaint was received from the 1300 block of Lincoln Avenue, where two domesticated ducks were reportedly in need of help. One duck was taken into custody.

Sept. 19

12:20 p.m. A woman in the 600 block of Sandhill Circle called to report that she was concerned about a dog on a deck that "looked like it wanted to jump."

Dec. 16

4:21 a.m. Police assisted a man in the 1000 block of Highpoint Drive who claimed to have been locked out of his room for three hours. Police said the man didn't know if the people he was sharing a room with were passed out or ignoring him.

· · · · · · · · · · · · · · · ·

Dec. 18

2:24 p.m. A suspicious incident was reported at the Bud Werner Memorial Library, where a person was accessing inappropriate material on a public computer. Police took a report.

· · · · · · · · · · · · · · · ·

Dec. 23

3:53 p.m. An unfounded automobile theft was reported in the 1900 block of Cornice Drive. A woman told police her car was stolen, but officers discovered the car covered in snow in the parking lot.

· · · · · · · · · · · · · · · ·

Dec. 24

11:13 a.m. A two-vehicle, noninjury accident was reported at the Steamboat Springs Police Department, where a fire truck backed into a patrol car. Police took a report.

· · · · · · · · 2008 · · · · · · · ·

March 26

11:39 p.m. A suspicious incident was reported in the 2400 block of Ski Trail Lane, where a shirtless man in the hallway of a condominium complex was frightening a group of girls. The man was simply working out and nothing was amiss.

Jan. 2

6:14 p.m. Residents in the 600 block of Gilpin Street reported a sleeping female elk was blocking access to a home. Police assisted the residents in getting the animal to move.

. . . .

Jan. 6

3:06 p.m. An elderly man reportedly stole creamer in the 200 block of Anglers Drive. The man was warned and asked to leave.

. . . .

Jan. 15

3:31 p.m. A suspicious incident was reported in Steamboat Springs, where a woman received an alarming text message. The message turned out to be religious in nature and was mistakenly sent to the recipient.

. . . .

Jan. 21

3:39 p.m. A suspicious incident was reported in the 2500 block of Liftline Way, where a babysitter thought someone was trying to break into a home. The person turned out to be a meter reader, and everything was fine.

. . . .

Jan. 25

9:07 a.m. A banjo and golf clubs found in the 100 block of Ninth Street were turned in to the Steamboat Springs Police Department.

Jan. 30

4:25 p.m. Two llamas were reported on Routt County Road 25 outside Oak Creek. The road was cleared.

. . . .

Feb. 19

10:27 a.m. A suspicious incident was reported in the 1400 block of 13th Street, where city transit officials received a threatening phone message. An intoxicated man who was dissatisfied with service threatened to cause a disturbance on a city bus and left a profanity-laced tirade against transit personnel. Police contacted the man and warned him never to use the city's bus service again. No charges were filed.

9:11 p.m. Trespassing was reported in the 2600 block of Burgess Creek Road, where second-home owners arrived at their residence to find other people inside. The people had the permission of a maintenance man to be in the residence. Police are investigating.

. . . .

Feb. 21

10:40 a.m. A woman locked herself out of a running vehicle with her child still inside. Police helped the woman unlock the car. Her child was fine.

. . . .

Feb. 23

9:03 p.m. A woman called police to report that a man said he had a bomb at a business in the 1800 block of Ski Time Square. The suspect said he was being sarcastic. Police said the object in question was a can of food.

. . . .

March 1

3:32 p.m. A man reported illegal dumping or littering on Routt County Road 25. He told the Sheriff's Office he thought someone was dumping dresser drawers into a ditch.

1:58 p.m. A vehicle was reported stolen from the 100 block of Ninth Street. Police said the driver's friend had moved the car around the corner to teach him a lesson about leaving his vehicle running with the keys in the ignition.

Feb. 1

March 3

1:22 p.m. A vehicle complaint was reported from Mount Werner Circle, where a man followed another driver into a parking lot and yelled obscenities at the driver after he had been honked at.

. . . .

March 6

7:19 a.m. An unfounded burglary report was received from the 2400 block of Lincoln Avenue, where employees found their business in disarray. The business' owner apparently made the mess to teach his employees a lesson after the doors were left unlocked Wednesday night, police said.

7:59 a.m. A suspicious incident was reported in the 100 block of Lincoln Avenue, where a passing motorist reported seeing two small children standing unattended on the sidewalk in their pajamas. When police arrived, the children were wearing ski clothes and were accompanied by their parents.

March 8

9:11 a.m. A person complained about animals in the 28400 block of Yellow Jacket Drive. Two dogs were reportedly chasing a cow elk. The dogs were taken into custody.

. . . .

March 16

2:22 p.m. Furniture was dumped in a no-dumping zone near mile marker 1 on Routt County Road 27 in Oak Creek. Authorities took a report.

4:51 p.m. A child lit a roll of toilet paper on fire in the 40000 block of Lindsay Drive. The fire was out when authorities arrived, and the residents ventilated the apartment.

. . . .

March 18

9:11 a.m. Police ticketed a man using his mother's season ski pass at Steamboat Ski Area.

. . . .

March 23

2:19 a.m. A man reported trespassing in progress when a group of people were climbing on a crane in a construction area near the base of the gondola. Police said the people were about four stories up on the construction equipment and were contacted on the way down.

March 26

9:50 a.m. Harassment was reported in the 2300 block of Abbey Road, where neighbors were bothering a woman because her baby was crying. Police took a report.

• • • • • • • • • • • • • • • •

April 1

9:28 p.m. A suspicious person was reported in the 1400 block of South Lincoln Avenue. A man was putting out cigarettes in flower pots, ripping leaves off plants, putting them in his car and handing them out to store customers. Police took a report.

• • • • • • • • • • • • • • • •

April 3

12:16 a.m. A bear was reported attempting to get into a residence in the 1700 block of Natches Way. The bear was trying to enter the garage through a dog door. Police shooed the bear away.

• • • • • • • • • • • • • • • •

April 12

7:16 p.m. Sheriff's Office deputies responded to a report of a small black pickup pulling teenagers behind it in a wheelchair and doing laps around Heritage Park. Officers contacted the juveniles and told them to stop, which they did.

• • • • • • • • • • • • • • • •

April 13

12:30 a.m. A man complained about yelling and loud music in the 700 block of North Grand Street but asked Steamboat Springs police not to contact the noisy parties because it doesn't seem to do any good. Police contacted the parties, but no action was taken.

• • • • • • • • • • • • • • • •

April 14

2:01 a.m. Vandalism was reported in the 2700 block of Village Drive, where police said a "happy face" had been spray-painted on a garage door. Police took a report.

April 21

11:34 p.m. A suspicious incident was reported in the 3000 block of Duckels Court. The caller heard what he thought was a person or an animal screaming. It turned out to be a fox.

• • • • • • • • • • • • • • • •

April 23

10:41 p.m. Harassment was reported in Steamboat Springs, where a woman's ex-boyfriend was outside her residence. The man had sent the woman about 100 text messages and was calling her nonstop, police said. The man was given a courtesy ride home.

• • • • • • • • • • • • • • • •

May 6

9:47 p.m. A suspicious incident was reported on Routt County Road 22. A Sheriff's Office spokeswoman said someone with a lit torch was along the road.

• • • • • • • • • • • • • • • •

May 12

6:08 p.m. Theft of a cat was reported in the 2900 block of West Acres Drive. A Steamboat Springs man, a former roommate of the cat's owner, was arrested on suspicion of second-degree burglary and theft. The cat was recovered and returned to its owner.

May 16

10:04 p.m. A male skateboarder who fled police dove into the Yampa River near 13th Street. After a nearly two-hour search of the river, the man was safely located at another location. Police issued a citation for skateboarding on the highway.

• • • • • • • • • • • • • • • •

May 17

4:36 p.m. A suspicious person was reported in the 2000 block of Mount Werner Circle. A man who had been relieving himself in a parking structure in Ski Time Square was contacted and told to use a more appropriate location.

• • • • • • • • • • • • • • •

May 20

9:43 p.m. A disturbance was reported in the 300 block of South Lincoln Avenue, where two people were yelling. The men were watching a basketball game, and everything was fine.

• • • • • • • • • • • • • • •

May 21

8:31 p.m. An animal complaint was received from the 3200 block of Aspen Wood Drive, where a bear entered a garage, dragged a trash can into the yard and began eating the refuse. Police encouraged the bear to move along with the aid of a few beanbag rounds.

May 23

2:46 a.m. A suspicious incident was reported on Whistler Road, where a group of juveniles put a wooden chair in the middle of the street and set it on fire. Everyone was gone when police arrived.

• • • • • • • • • • • • • • • •

May 28

4:10 p.m. A suspicious incident was reported on East Maple Street, where a boy reportedly was sitting in a vehicle with a rifle. The boy had purchased a new BB gun that day and was waiting for a friend to try out the new gun on private property. Police gave a warning about loading the weapon in a vehicle.

• • • • • • • • • • • • • • • •

June 1

1:07 a.m. A suspicious vehicle was reported in the 34900 block of U.S. Highway 40. Occupants of the vehicle said they stopped to look at the stars.

April 16

8:54 p.m. A bear was reported in a vehicle in the 2600 block of Ridge Road. A woman left the doors open while she was carrying groceries into the house. When she returned, a bear was in the car eating the food. Police chased off the animal.

11:26 a.m. A missing person was reported in the 300 block of Cherry Drive. A woman said her boyfriend had not come home in a couple of days. Officers found out it was because he had been in jail for a day or two.

June 8

June 20

11:06 p.m. A suspicious person was reported on Balsam Court, where he had been walking around in the street for an hour with a flashlight. The man was looking for his lost cat.

. . . .

June 22

1:39 a.m. A suspicious vehicle was reported at Pine Grove Road and the Mountain Fire Station. The vehicle was parked in the dark near the station. Police said "a couple of romantics in the vehicle were asked to take it somewhere else."

. . . .

June 28

8:56 p.m. Threats were reported in the 21800 block of Fourth Avenue in Phippsburg. Two neighbors were arguing. One complained about the other shooting his ducks. Both were issued trespassing tickets. A report was taken.

July 6

6:43 p.m. A noise complaint was reported in Brooklyn Park. The reporting person said there was a group of people passing around a bottle of whiskey and screaming profanities. Officers were unable to locate the group.

. . . .

July 7

12:57 p.m. A vehicle complaint was received from Huckleberry Lane, where an elderly man was parked in the middle of the road looking at a house for sale. When a woman who was unable to pass his vehicle asked him to move, he yelled at her to get a smaller car and punched her vehicle when she drove past. Sheriff's Office deputies took a report.

. . . .

July 9

1:13 p.m. A suspicious person was reported sitting in a parked vehicle in the 1400 block of Blue Spruce Court. The person was a meter-reader. Everything was fine.

. . . .

July 12

4:30 p.m. A Steamboat Springs Transit bus driver reported threats from a man who the driver would not let on the bus because of the large inner tube the man was carrying.

. . . .

July 14

9:54 a.m. A suspicious incident was reported in the 25600 block of Routt Street in Phippsburg, where bones were found in a sinkhole. The remains turned out to be those of a cow and horse.

July 16

9:10 p.m. A suspicious incident was reported in the 2200 block of Val D'Isere Circle, where a window had been broken and blinds ripped down at a residence. Police determined the damage was caused by a bear trying to enter the home and referred the situation to the Colorado Division of Wildlife.

July 21

8:16 a.m. A one-vehicle, rollover accident was reported near mile marker 3 on Routt County Road 27. A 29-year-old Oak Creek man, who was distracted because he was eating a doughnut, drove off the side of the road, rolling his vehicle at least three times, according to the Colorado State Patrol. He was transported to the hospital via ambulance with minor injuries and cited for careless driving.

Aug. 4

2:54 p.m. Police were called to the 1800 block of Central Park Drive, where a woman was unable to rebuff a man's advances. Police took a report.

Aug. 10

12:19 a.m. A suspicious incident was reported on County Road 80 near Hayden where a person in a black trench coat riding a black horse was reportedly chasing a man in a car. Routt County Sheriff's deputies were unable to locate the rider.

Aug. 4

11:08 p.m. A drunken driver was reported at Fourth and Pine streets, where a man pulled over after weaving, threw up on the side of the road and got back in his car. A bicyclist also reported nearly being hit by the same driver. Police were unable to locate the vehicle.

Aug. 5

9:43 a.m. A woman reportedly was trying to flag down other vehicles for help near mile marker 128 on U.S. Highway 40 near Steamboat II. Sheriff's Office deputies contacted the woman, and she said she was just waving at people.

Aug. 13

5:26 p.m. A boy reportedly was crying while riding his bicycle near Mount Werner Road and U.S. Highway 40. Police were unable to locate him.

Aug. 18

4:28 p.m. Assistance was requested in the 300 block of 11th Street, where a paraglider landed in a tree.

Aug. 21

12:44 a.m. Vandalism was reported in the 600 block of Lincoln Avenue, where a man wrote graffiti in a bathroom. A 23-year-old Fort Collins man, who was identified as the suspect because he wrote all over himself in a similar fashion, was arrested on suspicion of defacing property and second-degree assault after spitting on an officer during his arrest.

Sept. 2

7:25 a.m. An animal complaint was received from the 29200 block of Elk View Drive, where a neighbor's geese were trespassing onto adjoining property. Animal control officers contacted the owners.

Sept. 7

9:40 a.m. Several people complained about littering in the 1000 block of Meadow Lane. Several forks had been stabbed into their lawns.

· · · · · · · · · · · · · · · ·

Sept. 9

2:01 p.m. A suspicious person was reported on a bus in Steamboat Springs, where a man was riding around with no particular destination. The man was doing nothing criminal.

· · · · · · · · · · · · · · · ·

Oct. 5

2:14 p.m. Police responded to a report of a suspicious person in the 400 block of Tamarack Drive, where a man and a woman were screaming and cursing at people in the parking lot of their building. Both recently had been released from detox and both were sent back.

· · · · · · · · · · · · · · · ·

Oct. 11

2:15 a.m. An officer was requested in the 500 block of Anglers Drive. A man had locked himself out of his house and was scaling the building to get in.

· · · · · · · · · · · · · · · ·

Oct. 21

11:00 p.m. Suspicious vehicles were reported in the 2600 block of Copper Ridge Circle. Three men who had been drinking beer and working on their trucks reportedly were testing out their new suspensions in an adjacent field. Two of the drivers, both of Steamboat Springs, were arrested on suspicion of driving under the influence and DUI per se. The third driver was not intoxicated.

5:28 p.m. An animal complaint was received from the 55000 block of Routt County Road 62 in Clark, where a woman wanted to take her dog to the pound because it had killed four sheep and two ducks and had attacked a deer.

Sept. 9

Oct. 23

5:47 p.m. Shoplifting was reported in the 1800 block of Central Park Drive where a woman stole three Halloween costumes and a feather boa. The woman left the store before police arrived. Police took a report.

· · · · · · · · · · · · · · · ·

Nov. 2

4:28 p.m. Sheriff's Office deputies responded to a request for an officer in the 44200 block of Routt County Road 36 in Steamboat Springs, where someone complained about another person smoking in the Strawberry Park Hot Springs. A report was taken.

Nov. 8

10:25 a.m. Police responded to a wildlife call on the Yampa River Core Trail behind Fish Creek Mobile Home Park. They issued a verbal warning to a person who was fishing with live bait.

. . . .

Nov. 9

10:47 p.m. Police and Steamboat Springs Fire Rescue responded to a reported fire in the 1500 block of Shadow Run Court, where a couch was in flames on a sidewalk and two young males were taking pictures of the fire. Fire Rescue firefighters put out the flames when they arrived. Police said the cause of the fire appeared to be intentional, but it is not known who set it. The incident is under investigation.

. . . .

Nov. 15

8:57 p.m. Harassment was reported in the 200 block of Lincoln Avenue where a motel clerk was receiving unwanted advances from a guest. Police escorted the guest off the property to another hotel.

Nov. 16

1:13 a.m. Police responded to an anonymous request for an officer in the 600 block of Yampa Street. The reporting party said a group of underage people wearing 1980s outfits were drinking in a bar and were getting ready to fight. Officers were unable to find any underage drinkers, or anyone matching the 1980s description, when they arrived.

. . . .

Nov. 19

12:30 p.m. A missing person was reported in the 1800 block of Central Park Drive, where a woman lost her 74-year-old mother while shopping and could not locate her in any of the nearby stores. The missing woman had boarded a shuttle back to her condo and was safely located there.

5:59 p.m. A suspicious incident was reported in the 100 block of 10th Street where a man brought a large hunting knife to municipal court. Police took a report.

Nov. 16

1:28 a.m. Police and Routt County Sheriff's Office deputies responded to a disturbance in the 500 block of Lincoln Avenue and arrested a 24-year-old Delta man on suspicion of third-degree trespass, resisting arrest, drinking in violation of a restraint order and disorderly conduct. Police said the disturbance began when an officer was waved down to respond to someone trying to pick fights behind a Lincoln Avenue bar. The person causing the disturbance ran when he saw the officer and was chased through downtown until he ended up on a rooftop, where he shouted vulgarities to officers below. The man was arrested on the rooftop.

Nov. 21

6:05 p.m. A suspicious incident was reported in the 54100 block of Routt County Road 129 in Clark where a man refusing to leave a store threw four rolls of toilet paper at a clerk's head.

Dec. 5

2:46 p.m. A disturbance was reported in the 3400 block of Après Ski Way, where a woman reported her neighbor was pounding surveying stakes into her property and ramming his snowplow into her trees. Police took a report.

Dec. 7

10:33 a.m. Police responded to a request for an officer in Steamboat Springs, where a woman said a man walked into the front office of a lodging property and asked where he could find a strip club. A front desk employee gave the man a phone book, and he left. He came back soon after and exposed himself to the employee. The incident is under investigation, and a report was taken.

Dec. 8

2:02 p.m. Fraud was reported in the 300 block of Table Rock Road in McCoy, where someone registered for a MySpace account using someone else's identity. Routt County Sheriff's Office deputies took a report.

Dec. 10

12:54 p.m. Theft of a cellphone was reported in the 900 block of Central Park Drive. Whoever allegedly stole the phone about a week and a half prior had charged a $400 phone bill. Police took a report.

Dec. 10

4:23 p.m. An officer was requested in the 3100 block of Ingles Lane, where a man reported that a hotel front desk clerk refused to give personal property back. The hotel had confiscated a propane grill the man was using to cook food in his room. It was returned after police arrived.

6:50 p.m. A suspicious incident was reported on Hanover Street, where a flaming bag of dog feces was left on a woman's porch.

Dec. 15

8:38 p.m. A vehicle complaint was received from Milner where snowmobilers were racing on Spruce and Pine streets and Third Avenue. They were gone when Sheriff's Office deputies arrived.

Dec. 23

12:45 p.m. Theft of a package was reported on Maple Street, where a woman's neighbor refused to give her a package mistakenly delivered to the wrong house.

Dec. 6

7:38 a.m. A burglary was reported in the 200 block of Old Fish Creek Falls Road. A drunken person reportedly entered somebody's residence, put on their clothes and stole beverages from their refrigerator. An arrest was made.

· · · · · · · 2009 · · · · · · · ·

Nov. 2

5:38 p.m. Police were called to a report of a suspicious incident in the 2900 block of West Acres Drive, where a woman reported that she found feces in her toilet that she did not think she put there. There was no damage to the house and no other reason to believe someone had been inside the house.

Featured in "Headlines" segment on "The Jay Leno Show!"

Jan. 1

3:53 a.m. A domestic dispute was reported in Oak Creek where people were yelling at each other. The noise was New Year's revelers, and everything was fine.

• • • • • • • • • • • • • • • •

Jan. 6

7:23 a.m. A welfare check was requested on a woman in the alley between the 400 blocks of Oak and Pine streets. The woman was wearing open-toed shoes in the snow. Everything was fine.

• • • • • • • • • • • • • • • •

Jan. 7

6:41 p.m. A moose reportedly fell through ice on a pond in the 700 block of Anglers Drive. The Colorado Division of Wildlife was contacted, but the moose freed itself.

10:55 p.m. A disturbance was reported in the 2300 block of Mount Werner Circle, where about 150 people in line for a concert were being unruly and throwing snowballs. Police assisted with crowd control.

• • • • • • • • • • • • • • • •

Jan. 15

10:10 p.m. A 22-year-old Oak Creek man was reported missing by his girlfriend. The man was last seen that morning, when he was dropped off to snowboard at the Gondola Transit Center in Steamboat Springs. Routt County Search and Rescue and Steamboat Ski Patrol crews were ready to search for the man on Mount Werner on Friday, but the man eventually made it home safely early Friday morning. He had been unable to find a ride back to South Routt on Thursday and reportedly ended up walking and hitchhiking home.

Jan. 17

2:27 p.m. Police took a report of vandalism in the 1500 block of Clubhouse Drive, where a property owner had discovered fecal matter in a pool.

• • • • • • • • • • • • • • • •

Jan. 21

1:31 p.m. A two-vehicle, hit-and-run accident was reported at a parking lot on Mount Werner Circle. A woman reported that a man in a green truck hit her parked vehicle, but it did not cause damage. The man then reportedly yelled at the woman, called her names, told her she was parked illegally and sped away, spraying the woman with mud and rocks from the spinning tires.

• • • • • • • • • • • • • • • •

Jan. 23

12:17 a.m. A suspicious incident was reported in the 2100 block of Snow Bowl Plaza, where a woman's dogs were barking. According to the reporting person, the last time her dogs were barking like that, someone was trying to break into a business in the area. Everything was fine.

• • • • • • • • • • • • • • • •

Jan. 26

5:30 p.m. A muskrat at large was reported on Shield Drive. The animal was so cold that it was all curled up, according to the reporting person.

• • • • • • • • • • • • • • • •

Jan. 29

12:45 p.m. Harassment was reported in Steamboat Springs, where a woman reportedly accused her neighbor of yelling at her over the phone, and she further reportedly accused the woman of stealing her neighbor's newspaper. Police mediated the dispute.

Jan. 29

11:45 p.m. An assault was reported in the 700 block of Lincoln Avenue, where police said a woman pushed another woman off a stage. Police issued a harassment summons.

. . . .

Feb. 4

11:03 a.m. A 63-year-old Steamboat Springs man was arrested on suspicion of driving under revocation in the 1900 block of Shield Drive. People in the parking lot had seen the man acting strangely, throwing soda cans and newspapers under cars, as if he were upset. The man reportedly drove himself to court on a revoked license and was late for his fifth DUI sentencing earlier that morning.

. . . .

Feb. 7

1:46 p.m. An officer was requested in the 2100 block of Curve Plaza, where a person's laundry was locked inside a laundromat. Police told the person they would have to wait until the business reopened.

. . . .

Feb. 9

3:00 p.m. A man riding a city bus was reportedly making a drug deal on his cellphone. The man got off the bus before police arrived. Police took a report.

Feb. 9

6:23 p.m. A disturbance was reported in the 400 block of Tamarack Drive where a man and woman were arguing. The man had been shoveling snow out of a parking space and got angry when the woman pulled into it. Police mediated the dispute.

. . . .

Feb. 11

12:38 p.m. A resident in the 1300 block of Indian Trails reported that someone threw a cigarette butt in his or her driveway.

3:28 p.m. A suspicious incident was reported in the 700 block of Tamarack Drive, where people were seen loading a city street sign into a moving truck. Police confiscated the sign and took a report.

. . . .

Feb. 12

7:15 a.m. A disturbance was reported at Clubhouse and Overlook drives, where a woman and her grandson were arguing about his driving skills. He reportedly parked the car in a snow bank and ended up walking to the bus stop.

Jan. 10

1:49 a.m. Two 23-year-old men were arrested at the corner of Third Street and Lincoln Avenue. The two apparently were intoxicated and broke into a pickup. They proceeded to throw items out of the truck into the snow. They then inadvertently locked themselves in the cab of the truck and triggered the truck's alarm as they exited. An officer heard the car alarm and arrested the men.

7:50 a.m. A kitten was frozen to the sidewalk by its paws at Lincoln Avenue and Anglers Drive. The animal was stuck but breathing, the caller said. An animal control officer took the kitten to the shelter.

Feb. 8

Feb. 17
8:09 a.m. An animal complaint was received from Storm Meadows Drive, where a man left a dog unrestrained in the back of a pickup and went skiing. Animal control officers checked on the dog, and it was fine.

. . . .

Feb. 24
7:38 a.m. A fire was reported in the 200 block of Howelsen Parkway where smoke was seen coming from a pile of Christmas trees due for recycling. The smoke actually was steam from melting snow, and there was no fire.

3:23 p.m. A suspicious incident was reported in the 2400 block of Storm Meadows Drive, where a naked man was reported in the parking lot. Police were unable to locate him.

Feb. 25
11:59 a.m. A Bible was reported found in a parking lot off U.S. Highway 40 on Rabbit Ears Pass.

. . . .

Feb. 26
12:21 p.m. A suspicious incident was reported in the 1700 block of Central Park Drive, where a person with a concealed weapons permit accidentally dropped a handgun in a restaurant, causing it to discharge a bullet into the wall. No one was injured.

. . . .

March 1
7:13 p.m. A woman complained about a man dropping his pants and mooning her in the 1800 block of Central Park Drive. A report was taken.

. . . .

March 10
9:27 p.m. Officers were called to a residence in the 2300 block of Storm Meadows Drive, where two teenagers reportedly heard thumping and unusual noises from the front of the house and had locked themselves in a bathroom. Police responded and found everything was fine.

. . . .

March 11
9:30 p.m. Theft of a drain cover was reported from the 2000 block of Snow Bowl Plaza.

. . . .

March 17
7:21 a.m. Deputies responded to a report of a suspicious person in the 300 block of East First Street in Oak Creek, where a resident reported a person walking around with a clipboard. The person was reading meters, and everything was fine.

March 27

12:47 a.m. A suspicious person was reported at U.S. Highway 40 west of downtown Steamboat. A Routt County Sheriff's Office deputy stopped to ask a man walking on the road if he needed assistance, and the man hid and began running away along the Yampa River, according to law enforcement. The man could not be located.

. . . .

March 29

12:14 a.m. Steamboat Springs Police Department officers responded to a report of drunken pedestrians in the 600 block of Lincoln Avenue. Several people were reportedly laying in Lincoln Avenue for pictures and were not moving for oncoming cars. There was no report of their description, and officers were unable to find the group.

11:24 p.m. Police responded to a report of a theft in the 3000 block of Columbine Drive. Officers had initially contacted a reportedly drunken pedestrian who requested a taxi. Officers helped the man get a taxi, and when he arrived at his hotel, he walked in without paying for the ride. Officers again contacted the man, and he paid his fare. No charges were filed.

March 30

9:03 a.m. Police responded to a one-car, noninjury accident on the James Brown Soul Center of the Universe Bridge. Officers took a report.

4:08 p.m. Police responded to a suspicious incident at Walton Creek Road and South Lincoln Avenue where a group of people were seen wrapping an object in a blanket on the roadside. The group was gone when officers arrived.

. . . .

April 5

1:11 p.m. Police were called to a complaint in the first block of Anglers Drive, where a woman said that someone had altered a profile on her computer to state that she is a prostitute. Officers took a report.

2:16 p.m. Police were called to a complaint in the 800 block of Howelsen Parkway, where a person said it appeared children had cut down a tree near the BMX park and were building a fort. Officers contacted the juveniles.

. . . .

April 6

12:53 p.m. Police were called to a report of vandalism in the 1100 block of South Lincoln Avenue, where a car windshield was broken. Police discovered that a 38-pound rubber band ball apparently had been pushed down Ramada Inn Drive and struck the windshield of the car. Police took the rubber band ball into evidence.

. . . .

April 12

8:06 p.m. Deputies were called to a rescue at the top of Morningside Lift at Steamboat Ski Area, where deputies were trying to guide a man, suspected of being intoxicated, down the mountain.

April 14

4:42 p.m. Police were called to a report of a suspicious person in the 3600 block of Lincoln Avenue, where rocks were rolling into the road. Officers contacted two children on the hillside above who were digging a fort. Officers asked them to stop their digging, and they returned home.

. . . .

April 17

12:06 p.m. Police were called to a suspicious incident in the 2900 block of Heavenly View. A person reported finding a toilet that had been used in an unoccupied home and was concerned. Everything was fine.

. . . .

April 23

3:41 a.m. Police were called to a report of a bear in the 1900 block of Cornice Road, where a man walking his dogs reportedly was chased by a bear with two cubs. Officers urged the bear to return to the wilderness by shooting it with a beanbag round.

. . . .

May 1

2:43 a.m. A man reported a suspicious incident on Anglers Drive. Police said juveniles took a case of beer from a convenience store, left a $20 on the counter and fled. The juveniles could not be located.

May 3

11:32 p.m. Police were called to a report of a bear in the 2500 block of Anthony's Circle, where a 300-pound bear was reportedly banging on a window. The bear was gone when officers arrived.

. . . .

May 5

1:08 p.m. Police were called to a report of theft of a baby crib from the 500 block of Oak Street. The crib is valued at $125.

4:20 p.m. Deputies were called to a report of two llamas grazing in a neighbor's yard in the 26000 block of Neptune Place in Clark. The owner of the llamas was contacted, and the llamas were taken home.

. . . .

May 6

3:56 a.m. Police were called to a complaint of two men loudly playing with nunchucks outside in the first block of Spruce Street. Officers issued a verbal warning and asked the men to move inside.

. . . .

May 7

12:42 p.m. A semitrailer caught fire on U.S. Highway 40 at the base of Rabbit Ears Pass. No injuries were reported in the blaze, which started when the semi's engine overheated. The fire blocked traffic on U.S. 40 for several hours. The semi was carrying beer to a local distributor.

. . . .

May 11

3:17 p.m. Police were called to a request for an officer in the 300 block of Lincoln Avenue, where a customer was not pleased with service from a bank. Officers reminded the man it was a private business and that he could choose to take his business elsewhere.

May 11

4:28 p.m. Police were called to a report of a theft of a cowboy hat, valued at $250, from the first block of Anglers Drive.

9:39 p.m. While police were responding to another call nearby, officers were alerted to a theft in progress in the 1400 block of South Lincoln Avenue, where a man reportedly grabbed two cases of Budweiser beer from a liquor store and ran away. A manager gave chase, and an officer arrested a 20-year-old Steamboat Springs man on suspicion of theft and being a minor in possession of alcohol. The beer was returned to the store.

. . . .

May 13

12:51 a.m. Steamboat Springs Police Department officers contacted a suspicious person at Fish Creek Falls Road and Amethyst Drive, where a man reportedly was carrying a knife. The man said he was a chef and that he was carrying the knife in case he was confronted by a bear. Officers gave the man a ride to his house.

May 13

6:30 a.m. Police were called to a suspicious incident at Steamboat Springs High School, where a custodian suspected a person was camping on the school lawn. The person was actually a teacher preparing for a lesson, and everything was fine.

. . . .

May 19

6:53 a.m. Police were called to a report of a "Burrito Babes" pickup stolen from the 1500 block of Meadow Lane. Officers took a report.

10:23 p.m. Police were called to a report of a bear in the 1500 block of Mark Twain Lane, where a bear apparently broke into a house through a screen window while the homeowners were away. The bear reportedly ate brownies, powdered sugar and honey from a bear-shaped honey bottle. The bear was gone by the time the homeowners returned.

May 19

May 26

1:23 p.m. Police were called to a report of an animal bite in the 3000 block of Village Drive, where a real estate agent, who was showing a house, was reportedly bitten by a cat.

10:21 p.m. Police were contacted by a person at Seventh Street and Lincoln Avenue for a report of two men fighting. The men were wrestling, and everything was fine.

• • • • • • • • • • • • • • •

June 3

6:55 p.m. Police were called to a report of theft of a golden retriever-shaped lawn ornament valued at about $200 from the 1600 block of Steamboat Boulevard.

• • • • • • • • • • • • • • •

June 14

12:15 p.m. Deputies responded to a report of a suspicious person in the area of mile marker 143 of U.S. Highway 40 in Steamboat. The person was picking ferns.

• • • • • • • • • • • • • • •

June 17

10:30 p.m. Police were called to a report of a suspicious incident in the 700 block of South Lincoln Avenue. A man reportedly called a hotel and asked to be transferred to a room. The caller told the guest in the room that there was a gas leak in the building and that in order to be safe, the guest needed to place a wet towel at the base of the door and use the back of the toilet tank to smash out the window. The guest smashed the window, but there was no gas leak. Officers are investigating.

• • • • • • • • • • • • • • •

June 23

2:29 p.m. Police were called to a report of vandalism in the 400 block of Lincoln Avenue, where someone spray-painted "no parking" on a car's windows. Officers took a report.

June 27

8:26 p.m. A juvenile situation was reported in the 800 block of Howelsen Parkway after some youths reportedly yelled profanities. They were given a warning.

• • • • • • • • • • • • • • •

June 29

10:03 a.m. Police were called to a report of a disturbance in the 100 block of Lincoln Avenue, where a customer in a store reportedly threw water at employees. The customer was gone when officers arrived.

• • • • • • • • • • • • • • •

June 30

6:49 a.m. Police were called to a report of fraud in the 400 block of Lincoln Avenue, where a business reportedly received a fax claiming to be from a dying Saudi Arabian merchant.

9:47 a.m. Police were called to a report of threats in the 1100 block of Hilltop Parkway, where people were arguing about the noise made by a document-shredding truck.

• • • • • • • • • • • • • • •

July 2

3:07 p.m. A person complained about a "beautiful gray cat hanging out for a few days."

July 7

4:36 p.m. Police were called to a cold report of theft in the 2700 block of Eagleridge Drive. A woman from Texas, who had been in Steamboat Springs recently, reportedly realized her Rolex watch was stolen from her car. The watch was reportedly insured for $19,000. Officers took a report.

· · · · · · · · · · · · · · · ·

July 8

10:56 p.m. Two people reportedly were having sex in the back of a dark green station wagon on Anglers Drive. The reporting party confronted the people in the car, which led to a shoving match. The unidentified man who was in the car left the scene before officers arrived. No charges are pending, according to police.

· · · · · · · · · · · · · · · ·

July 9

4:52 p.m. A homeowner in the 1900 block of Montview Court got into an argument with construction workers he accused of stealing his electricity. Officers mediated the situation, and the homeowner was given $5 to compensate for the use of electricity.

· · · · · · · · · · · · · · · ·

July 12

1:48 a.m. Two men wearing tuxedos reportedly were fighting near a parking garage in the 2300 block of Mount Werner Circle. The men were part of a wedding party. No charges were filed.

July 12

10:05 p.m. Police warned a group of eight people who were screaming, yelling and hula-hooping in a parking lot in the 700 block of Yampa Street.

· · · · · · · · · · · · · · · ·

July 13

4:12 a.m. Officers assisted Steamboat Springs Fire Rescue during an ambulance call to the 2200 block of Ski Time Square Drive. A 65-year-old woman who mistakenly swallowed a big swig of hydrogen peroxide, thinking it was water, was transported to Yampa Valley Medical Center.

12:44 p.m. Damage was reported to metal artwork in the 1500 block of Lincoln Avenue. The artwork, a sheep, was pulled from the ground and knocked over, but it was not damaged. A metal sheep was stolen from the same location the previous week.

· · · · · · · · · · · · · · · ·

July 18

6:07 p.m. Young children were reported throwing rocks at tubers on the Yampa River near 11th Street. Officers contacted their parents.

8:05 p.m. A theft was reported on the Yampa River near the A-Hole.

July 13

1:45 p.m. A Superman mannequin was stolen from an outdoor phone booth in the 600 block of South Lincoln Avenue. The incident is under investigation.

7:47 p.m. A bull was running loose on Conestoga Circle near the Pioneer Village subdivision. The bull was located, but its owner was unable to catch it before dark. The owner said he would try again the next morning. There was no information available the next day about whether he was successful.

July 21

July 20

8:29 p.m. Deputies were called to a report of harassment in the 40000 block of Anchor Way, where a woman was concerned about a person who approached her son in a parking lot. The person was handing out Bibles, and everything was fine.

. . . .

July 23

3:49 p.m. Police were called to a report of a shoplifter in Central Park Plaza, where a woman reportedly took several shopping carts full of groceries, totaling nearly $1,000, from a grocery store. Officers arrested a 31-year-old Steamboat woman on suspicion of theft.

5:45 p.m. Deputies were called to a report of a drunken driver near mile marker 4 on Routt County Road 129. Deputies found the driver was a young woman learning to drive and that she was not intoxicated. Deputies issued a warning.

July 26

12:03 a.m. A disturbance was reported in the first block of Seventh Street. A man who had been kicked out of a bar kept sneaking back in through the back door. The man was warned.

. . . .

July 28

8:17 p.m. Police were called to a request for an officer at Steamboat Springs High School, where people walking on the track reportedly had been locked in by a gate. The people were let out, and everything was fine.

. . . .

July 30

9:26 p.m. Police were called to a report of a disturbance in the 400 block of Howelsen Parkway, where a woman reportedly was trying to untie a couple of horses and was acting strangely. Officers asked the woman to leave.

. . . .

Aug. 13

10:50 p.m. Deputies were called to a report of a suspicious incident at Dodge and Moffat streets in Oak Creek, where a person reported a wheelchair in a ditch. The wheelchair was gone when deputies arrived.

. . . .

Aug. 14

8:28 a.m. Police were called to reports of vandalism on a median at Mount Werner Road. Someone broke all the branches off a crab apple tree.

. . . .

Aug. 19

4:26 p.m. Deputies were called to a report of a suspicious person in the 1100 block of Routt County Road 74 near Hayden, where a woman reported that a man walked up her driveway but left when she turned the light on. Deputies determined the man was a neighbor looking for his dog, and everything was fine.

Aug. 23

9:56 a.m. Routt County Sheriff's Office deputies were called to a report of a burglary in the 40000 block of Lindsay Drive, where an antique phone reportedly was stolen from a house.

3:39 p.m. Police were called to a welfare check in the 800 block of Lincoln Avenue, where store workers reported an intoxicated woman in a dressing room, and they said they were concerned for her safety. Officers took the woman to detox.

. . . .

Aug. 25

5:03 p.m. Police were called to a report of a disturbance in the 800 block of Lincoln Avenue, where a man reportedly left a restaurant without paying a bar tab, which totaled about $50. The man reportedly returned and attempted to pay with an invalid credit card, then attempted to leave again. Officers arrested a 50-year-old Steamboat man on suspicion of defrauding an innkeeper.

. . . .

Aug. 26

6:17 p.m. Police were called to a cold report of a theft in the 500 block of Seventh Street, where a pottery kiln, valued at about $300, reportedly was stolen during a garage sale.

2:34 p.m. Police were called to a report of a suspicious incident near the Yampa River, where a man was reportedly taking pictures of children. Officers found the man was a photographer and artist and that everything was fine.

. . . .

Aug. 30

2:23 a.m. Police contacted three people on Yampa Street between Fifth and Sixth streets, where a man and two women were running and hiding. The three were playing hide-and-seek.

Aug. 30

10:20 a.m. Police were called to a request for an officer in the 500 block of Wyatt Way for an ongoing dispute between neighbors. One resident reportedly spray-painted "eat me" on a section of his shed that faces his neighbor's property. Officers tried to mediate the situation.

. . . .

Sept. 7

1:23 a.m. Steamboat Springs Police Department officers were called to a noise complaint in the alley behind the 700 block of Lincoln Avenue, where a woman was "hooting and hollering," according to the report. Police found three or four people reportedly being loud and gave them a verbal warning.

. . . .

Sept. 9

12:46 a.m. Steamboat Springs Police Department officers were called to a report of a suspicious person at 13th and Gilpin streets, where a man who reportedly appeared to be in his early 20s was reported walking back and forth in the middle of the street.

Sept. 9

5:43 p.m. Police were called to a complaint about a car driving near Hilltop Parkway and U.S. Highway 40 with "for sale" signs in the window. The caller was concerned the driver's view was obscured. Officers were unable to find the car.

· · · · · · · · · · · · · · · ·

Sept. 13

4:04 a.m. Deputies were called to a report of a stolen vehicle in the 100 block of West Virginia Street in Oak Creek. Deputies said the car was taken on a joy ride and returned.

· · · · · · · · · · · · · · · ·

Sept. 14

11:39 a.m. Police were called to a report of theft of cash in Central Park Plaza, where a person reported they accidentally put $200 through a movie drop box. The money was later missing. Officers took a report and are investigating.

· · · · · · · · · · · · · · · ·

Sept. 17

3:18 p.m. Deputies were called to a report of a suspicious incident in the 21000 block of Routt County Road 56 near Clark, where a person reportedly was looking for cattle growth hormone. Deputies took a report.

Sept. 27

1:23 a.m. Police were called to a report of a disturbance in the 2600 block of Copper Ridge Circle, where a woman reportedly was throwing skateboards out of a window and spitting on people. Officers mediated the situation and gave two people courtesy rides to Dream Island Mobile Home Park.

· · · · · · · · · · · · · · · ·

Oct. 7

9:40 a.m. Police were called to reports of a stray dog at Merritt Street and Yahmonite Road. A male pit bull reportedly broke loose and was dragging a chain from its neck. The dog was faster than the police officer, who was unable to catch the dog.

· · · · · · · · · · · · · · · ·

Oct. 13

10:21 a.m. Police were called to a complaint about a cat at large in the 600 block of Lincoln Avenue, where a kitten was reportedly living in a garbage bin.

· · · · · · · · · · · · · · · ·

Oct. 15

1:27 p.m. Police were called to a civil complaint in the 600 block of Lincoln Avenue. A person who drove away from a gas station with the hose still in the tank, which broke it off, returned to pay for the damage.

Sept. 19

7:06 p.m. Police were dispatched to a report of a person leaving bones and meat outside to bait a bear in the 400 block of Tamarack Drive. The case was referred to animal control.

Oct. 21

5:41 a.m. Police were called to a report of a suspicious incident at Steamboat Springs Airport, where a person reported flashing lights on the runway. The person thought that the lights might be from a plane that had crashed, but the lights are part of the runway system.

. . . .

Oct. 22

12:18 p.m. Deputies were called to a report of a suspicious incident in the 33000 block of Filly Trail outside of Oak Creek and Yampa, where a faucet reportedly was turned on and the basement of a home was flooded. Deputies are investigating.

. . . .

Oct. 25

7:56 a.m. Police were called to a report of a picnic table in the pond in West Lincoln Park in the 1300 block of Lincoln Avenue. Public works department employees were going to retrieve and repair the table.

. . . .

Oct. 26

3:00 p.m. Police were called to a request for an officer in the 2100 block of Mount Werner Road, where a woman reportedly was locked in a car wash when the front door of the car wash would not open. The woman was reluctant to get out of her car, and an attendant was contacted to open the car wash door.

. . . .

Oct. 27

10:58 a.m. Police were called to a report of a shoplifter in the first block of Anglers Drive, where a 16-year-old boy reportedly stole two bags of beef jerky from a convenience store. The boy's mother reportedly brought him back to the store, and an officer issued him a "promise to appear," a summons for juveniles.

Nov. 4

10:03 a.m. Deputies were called to a report of a car crash near mile marker 23 on Routt County Road 129, where a person reportedly hit a cow. The cow was fine and returned to a pasture.

. . . .

Nov. 10

10:45 a.m. Police were called to a report of vandalism in the 300 block of Primrose Lane, where a dog leash reportedly was cut into three pieces.

. . . .

Nov. 11

1:28 p.m. Police were called to a report of a suspicious incident near Rotary Park, where a man's dog reportedly found a beer bottle, a vodka bottle and a pair of women's underpants.

2:12 p.m. Police were called to a report of harassment. A woman had reportedly received pornographic images on her cellphone.

. . . .

Nov. 15

3:24 p.m. Police were called to a report of a car crash in Central Park Plaza, where someone reportedly took a tan Subaru wagon that was parked with the keys inside and crashed it into a concrete planter.

Nov. 19

6:21 p.m. Police were called to a report of a porcupine causing problems on Howelsen Hill.

. . . .

Nov. 21

6:32 p.m. Police arrested a 28-year-old Steamboat man on suspicion of theft in the 1900 block of Cornice Drive. The intoxicated man reportedly skipped out on a more than $20 taxi fare after trying to pay with $2 and a bad credit card. Officers told the man he could pay or go to jail. The man said he'd rather go to jail.

. . . .

Nov. 22

4:43 p.m. Police were called to a report of a juvenile driving a go-kart on a frozen pond in the 2700 block of South Lincoln Avenue. Officers warned the juveniles that driving on the pond was a bad idea.

. . . .

Nov. 23

1:14 a.m. Police were called to a report of a suspicious incident in the 200 block of Hill Street, where a woman reported that she heard a strange noise outside her house but could not see anything from her window. Officers determined that the noise was made by ice falling from her roof onto a trash can, and everything was fine.

. . . .

Nov. 24

4:07 p.m. Police were called to a request for an officer on West End Avenue, where children reportedly were being unruly on a Steamboat Springs School District bus. An officer and a school district supervisor spoke to the children about their behavior, and the bus continued after about a half-hour.

Nov. 30

11:15 a.m. Police were called to a report of ducks in the road in the 1300 block of Lincoln Avenue. One duck reportedly was killed in traffic, and two ducks returned to the pond.

. . . .

Dec. 1

2:50 a.m. Steamboat Springs Police Department officers stopped to help a motorist who was changing a flat tire in a parking lot in the 200 block of Lincoln Avenue. Officers found that the 21-year-old Leadville man had an outstanding warrant, and they arrested him.

8:19 p.m. Police were called to a report of a suspicious incident in the 600 block of Mountain Village Circle, where a woman reported that she was concerned because her husband left and she heard police sirens. Police found the man in his car in the area, and everything was fine.

. . . .

Dec. 3

10:43 a.m. Police were called to a report of a hit-and-run crash in the Yampa Valley Medical Center parking lot, where a person reportedly hit cars on either side of a parking space when she tried to park. She then left the space and parked in another spot. A bystander witnessed the incident and called police. Officers found the woman and issued her a ticket for failing to give notice after striking unattended cars.

4:52 p.m. Police were called to a disturbance in the 1200 block of Lincoln Avenue. A 5-year-old outside of a car was yelling and screaming. Officers made contact with the parents, who told officers their 5-year-old was upset for not being allowed to chew gum in the car.

Nov. 21

Dec. 6

6:27 p.m. Police were called to a report of a suspicious incident in the 3200 block of Après Ski Way, where a man reportedly gave two female neighbors a gift they did not appreciate. Officers told the man the gift was not well received.

. . . .

Dec. 7

9:03 a.m. Police were called to a report of a shoplifter in Central Park Plaza, where a woman reportedly was caught stealing a $15 wreath. The matter was handled by the store, and officers were not required.

Dec. 7

12:48 p.m. Police got a complaint from a woman in Steamboat that someone would not give her snow tires back to her until she returned a pair of sunglasses. The woman didn't know what sunglasses the person was talking about. Officers mediated the situation.

. . . .

Dec. 9

12:38 a.m. Steamboat Springs Police Department officers were called to a report of three or four men playing with the green plastic dinosaur at the gas station in the 2100 block of Mount Werner Road. Officers talked to the men and gave them a warning.

. . . .

Dec. 15

3:42 a.m. Police were called to a request for a welfare check on a woman who was painting a condo and had not returned to her home on Cypress Court for more than eight hours. Officers said the woman fell asleep after painting the room and that everything was fine.

6:22 a.m. Police were called to a report of a noise complaint and request for a welfare check in the 1300 block of Athens Plaza, where a man was reportedly yelling profanities and screaming. Officers checked on the man, and he reportedly said he had a bad dream.

. . . .

Dec. 16

8:53 a.m. Deputies served two warrants in the Yampa area and reportedly found about 58 marijuana plants in one of the homes. Deputies arrested a 61-year-old Phippsburg woman on suspicion of cultivating marijuana.

8:53 a.m. Police were called to a report of a suspicious incident in the 2100 block of Mount Werner Circle, where a man reported that someone was following him. Officers said the person following the man was a private investigator who was not being very covert.

Dec. 20

12:47 p.m. Police were called to a request for an officer in the 3000 block of Village Drive. Police said two people were arguing over laundry in a condo complex washroom. The argument began after one of them removed the other's laundry from a washing machine. The two made up.

. . . .

Dec. 21

4:07 p.m. Police were called to a request for a welfare check at Pine Grove Road and U.S. Highway 40, where a man waiting for a haircut reportedly was intoxicated and passed out. Officers took the man to detox.

. . . .

Dec. 22

12:06 p.m. Police were called to a report of an argument in the 2700 block of Eagleridge Drive, where two women were reportedly arguing about a parking place, and one woman reportedly pushed the other out of an elevator. There were no injuries, and neither woman wanted to press charges.

2:59 p.m. Police were called to a report of a woman in a sun hat and dress hitchhiking and jumping into traffic at U.S. Highway 40 and Shield Drive. The woman was gone when officers arrived.

Dec. 23

9:11 p.m. Deputies, Colorado Highway Patrol troopers and Oak Creek Fire Rescue emergency responders were called to a car crash at mile marker 57 on Colorado Highway 131. Deputies arrested a 31-year-old Steamboat man on suspicion of driving under the influence and weaving after his car slid off the road and down a 50-foot embankment. When deputies and troopers arrived, the man was waiting outside his car smoking a cigarette.

. . . .

Dec. 29

6:13 a.m. Police were dispatched to a wildlife call at Walton Creek Road and U.S. Highway 40. A moose was in the intersection slipping on the ice. Officers shooed it away.

. . . .

Dec. 30

10:25 p.m. Police were called to a request for a welfare check in the 3100 block of South Lincoln Avenue, where a man, set to be married the next day, reportedly became intoxicated and ran away. Officers were unable to find the person who called in the request or the groom-to-be.

Nov. 26

7:36 a.m. Police and Steamboat Springs Fire Rescue were called to a request for citizen assistance in the first block of Anglers Drive, where a person was having difficulty leaving his or her home because the doors were frozen shut. Firefighters helped open the door.

· · · · · · · · 2010 · · · · · · · ·

March 3

6:31 p.m. Police were called to a report of a suspicious incident in the 1000 block of Lincoln Avenue, where two men, described as large and covered in tattoos, reportedly put their fingers on the hand of another passenger while riding a bus.

11:39 p.m. Police were called to a report of a fight among three men in the 1800 block of Ski Time Square Drive. Officers talked to two of the men but could not find the third. The third man was described as a having a mohawk and wearing pink panties over his pink snow pants. Officers could not find the man.

Jan. 7

Jan. 4

9:20 a.m. Steamboat Springs Police Department officers were called to a report of a theft in the 500 block of Oak Street, where a church reported several figures from a Nativity scene were stolen. The figures were valued at several hundred dollars.

. . . .

Jan. 8

10:03 p.m. Police were called to a reported theft in the 2200 block of Village Inn Court. Someone appeared to have taken a large stuffed polar bear from the lobby of a hotel and run away with it, police said. Officers were unable to locate the bear or its suspected thief. An officer was unsure of the bear's monetary value.

Jan. 10

3:10 p.m. Police were called to a report that a squirrel was stuck in a stovepipe in the 800 block of Aspen Street. Police said they didn't know what happened to the squirrel.

. . . .

Jan. 15

12:49 a.m. Police were called to a suspicious person in Wildhorse Marketplace. Someone was climbing on the large horse sculpture at the shopping center, police said. Officers issued that person a warning.

. . . .

Jan. 20

12:29 p.m. Police were called to a report of a suspicious incident in the first block of Arapahoe Lane, where a person reportedly was walking door to door selling hand sanitizer. Officers got a similar call from another location later in the day but did not talk to the seller.

8:00 p.m. Police were called to a report of an apparently drunken hitchhiker near a bus stop in the 300 block of South Lincoln Avenue. The man reportedly was holding two helium balloons and wearing a work jacket and stepped in front of cars. The man was gone when officers arrived.

9:50 p.m. Police were called to a report of a suspicious incident in the 3300 block of Après Ski Way. A woman reported that her upstairs neighbors had started drilling holes through their floor into her living room, bedroom and kitchen area to spy on her. She reported that the people were also "getting heroin into her system via these portals." She told police a maintenance man had sealed the portals once but they had returned. Officers checked the house and determined that the report was unfounded.

Jan. 25

2:42 p.m. Police were called to a report of trespassing in the 300 block of Pine Street, where a woman reported that someone entered her car and smoked a cigarette. The woman reportedly knew the suspect, and nothing was missing from the car.

. . . .

Feb. 8

9:30 p.m. Police were called to a report of fraud in the 1800 block of Loggers Lane. A person in Florida reported that someone had impersonated him and bought $5,700 worth of carpet. Police are investigating.

. . . .

Feb. 13

3:13 p.m. Police arrested a 27-year-old Craig man on a felony charge of marijuana cultivation and misdemeanor charges of harassment and false imprisonment after being contacted by Steamboat Ski and Resort Corp. security in the Knoll parking lot on Mount Werner Circle. Police said Ski Corp. security saw the man leave a 3-foot-tall black trash bag near the parking area's security station. The bag contained full-grown marijuana plants still in potting soil, police said. Police said the man also allegedly harassed housekeeping staff at nearby condos. The incident is under investigation.

. . . .

Feb. 23

4:16 p.m. Police were called to a report of fraud in the 900 block of Lincoln Avenue, where a person reported that someone had ordered $5,000 worth of sparkling wine with a fraudulent credit card.

. . . .

March 4

2:49 p.m. Police were called to a report of a suspicious incident in Central Park Plaza, where a person working in a business reported that a man came in, slapped him and told him not to sell cocaine to his daughter. Officers took a report.

March 7

10:19 p.m. Police were called to a report of a suspicious incident in the 600 block of Hilltop Parkway, where a woman reported she thought she heard a loud boom or explosion coming from downtown that shook her house. Before officers could respond, the woman called back to say the sound was caused by snow and ice sliding off her roof, and everything was fine.

. . . .

March 9

4:35 a.m. Police were called to a report of a suspicious incident in the 1000 block of Lincoln Avenue where a person reported hearing something that sounded like Morse code, possibly from a skier. Officers found that the sound was coming from a building alarm, and everything was fine.

Feb. 21

3:11 a.m. Police were called to a report of a suspicious incident in the 2700 block of Eagleridge Drive, where a person reported that he or she could see a person in the bushes and hear two or three others. The people in the bushes reportedly were talking about how they were trying to crawl onto a balcony. The people were gone when officers arrived.

March 16

3:26 p.m. Police were called to a report of a suspicious incident in downtown Steamboat, where a woman reported that she saw two women and a man walking downtown and she thought they looked suspicious. She said she did not see them do anything specifically, but she had a feeling. The three people were gone when officers arrived, but they talked to the woman who called.

• • • • • • • • • • • • • • • •

March 19

10:03 a.m. Police were called to a report of lost property in the 3100 block of Après Ski Way. Someone reported losing $460 when strong winds blew the money away, police said.

• • • • • • • • • • • • • • • •

March 29

11:59 a.m. Police were called to the 2900 block of Columbine Drive, where somebody reportedly broke two fire extinguisher panels, took the two fire extinguishers and discharged them into a hot tub at a condo complex. A soap dispenser also was reported missing.

March 30

9:56 p.m. Police were called to a report of a domestic dispute, where a person heard neighbors yelling. Officers talked to the people involved and determined that the sound was from two people having sex.

• • • • • • • • • • • • • • • •

April 5

8:41 a.m. Police were called to a report of a suspicious incident in the 400 block of Anglers Drive, where a person reported finding a possible trail of blood. Officers determined that the substance was likely red grease.

• • • • • • • • • • • • • • • •

April 8

11:53 p.m. Police were called to the 800 block of Weiss Circle, where a woman reported that she was locked out of her apartment and there was a cake in the oven. Officers contacted a person with access to the apartment.

• • • • • • • • • • • • • • • •

April 16

9:38 p.m. Police were called to a report of animal bites in the 1400 block of Flattop Circle. A man reported being bitten on the hand by a fox while he was trying to feed the fox, police said. Officers turned over the case to the Colorado Division of Wildlife.

• • • • • • • • • • • • • • • •

April 25

5:48 p.m. Police were called to a request for an officer at Après Ski Way and Longthong Road, where a man reported that children were playing with a remote-controlled car in the street. The children were gone when officers arrived.

• • • • • • • • • • • • • • • •

May 3

12:39 p.m. Deputies were called to a complaint about two skinny horses in the 5400 block of Routt County Road 129 near Clark.

1:19 p.m. Police were called to a report of theft in Central Park Plaza. A man who reportedly was seen stealing an 18-pack of beer two hours earlier had returned to the grocery store and was reportedly walking out of the store with a jar of tartar sauce. When officers searched the man's bag, they discovered he also was attempting to steal a box of fish sticks. The 22-year-old Steamboat Springs man had been booked into jail on May 5 on a warrant and had been out of jail for two days before this incident.

May 12

May 16

4:25 p.m. Police were called to a report of two children, about 6 to 8 years old, playing with matches near brush at Alpenglow Way and Val d'Isere Circle.

. . . .

May 18

7:11 p.m. Police were called to a report of a young girl loudly blowing a whistle in West Acres Mobile Home Park. The girl reportedly was blowing the whistle earlier in the week, as well. Officers determined the girl was playing with an emergency whistle given out by Routt County Search and Rescue volunteers during school visits. Officers talked to the girl and her mother and told the girl the whistle was meant only for emergencies.

. . . .

May 19

7:36 p.m. Deputies found that someone put methamphetamine in the jail drop box, in a prescription bottle addressed to an inmate.

May 20

1:02 a.m. Police were called to a report of bears in the river near the 700 block of Yampa Street. Police watched the bears fish and swim, then leave the area.

. . . .

May 27

8:49 p.m. Police were called to a complaint about a car with several juveniles in the 800 block of Howelsen Parkway. People reportedly were jumping from the car while it was moving and riding on the hood. Police issued the driver a ticket.

. . . .

May 29

3:13 p.m. A man reported a burglary in the 1300 block of Dream Island Plaza. Police said a faucet valued at about $90 was stolen from a home. No other items were taken.

May 31

11:11 p.m. Police were called to a report of two men on playground equipment who were being loud in the 200 block of Park Avenue. Officers warned the men.

· · · · · · · · · · · · · · · ·

June 1

8:36 a.m. Police were called to a report of a disturbance in the 100 block of 10th Street, where a person at Steamboat Springs City Hall reportedly was unhappy about a water bill. Officers mediated the situation.

4:34 p.m. Police were called to a report of a disturbance on Whistler Road, where a person reportedly heard slamming and shouting. Officers determined that the noises were from a man and a woman moving a washing machine, and the machine was dropped on the woman's foot.

· · · · · · · · · · · · · · · ·

June 6

12:58 a.m. Police were called to a report of a suspicious car on Boulder Ridge. Officers determined it was a person taking pictures of the stars, and everything was fine.

June 9

8:52 p.m. Police were called to a noise complaint regarding a person mowing grass in the 900 block of Merritt Street. Police talked to the man mowing grass, and he voluntarily stopped.

· · · · · · · · · · · · · · · ·

June 11

9:57 p.m. Steamboat police were called to a juvenile situation. A caller reported that juveniles on the west end of town were pretending they had a rope stretched across the highway and trying to stop cars. They were gone when officers arrived.

· · · · · · · · · · · · · · · ·

June 14

10:09 p.m. Police were called to a report of a fawn unable to cross a guardrail on Burgess Creek Road.

· · · · · · · · · · · · · · · ·

June 15

6:58 p.m. Police were called to a report of a ring stolen from the 2200 block of Golf View Way. The owner was away on vacation and suspects the ring may have been taken during an open house. The ring was valued at $35,000.

July 14

1:45 p.m. Police were called to a report of a parakeet loose in Central Park Plaza. Officers determined that it was an African gray parrot that belonged to business owners nearby, and the bird was allowed to sit in a tree outside. Everything was fine.

June 17

8:28 p.m. Police were called to a report of an apparently intoxicated man in his 60s in the 400 block of South Lincoln Avenue. The man, wearing only underwear, was reportedly trying to sleep in a flower bed.

• • • • • • • • • • • • • • • •

June 29

9:37 a.m. Police were called to a report of a fishing net stolen from a vehicle in the 500 block of Yampa Street.

• • • • • • • • • • • • • • • •

July 2

1:14 p.m. Police were called to assist a person on the Yampa River Core Trail near Trafalgar Drive. Officers said a woman reported that a naked man in the weeds by the river was "conducting a sexual act on himself." Officers were unable to locate the man and didn't receive any other similar reports.

• • • • • • • • • • • • • • • •

July 6

1:01 p.m. Police were called to a report of a pug running in fresh asphalt on Bear Drive.

11:17 p.m. Police were called to a report of a suspicious car at the base of Howelsen Hill. Officers found a group of people playing volleyball after dark and asked them to leave.

• • • • • • • • • • • • • • • •

July 11

3:23 a.m. Routt County Sheriff's Office deputies and police were called to a report of vandalism in the 1200 block of Lincoln Avenue. Officers on foot patrol found a window broken at the Bud Werner Memorial Library. As they checked the inside of the building, they found a beer can, a pair of sunglasses and what could be drops of blood near the broken glass. There was no other damage inside the library.

July 12

5:28 p.m. Police were called to a report of teens drinking out of a whiskey bottle at 10th and Yampa streets. The teens were gone when officers arrived.

7:12 p.m. Police were called to a report of juveniles shooting at birds with a BB gun on West End Avenue. Officers warned the juveniles and their parents.

9:21 p.m. Police were called to a complaint about the public address system at the soccer field being too loud in the 1000 block of Eagle Glen Drive. Everything was fine when officers arrived.

• • • • • • • • • • • • • • • •

July 15

4:00 p.m. Police were called to a report of a theft at the St. Cloud Mountain Club. A manager reported that a bar stool valued at $2,500 was stolen July 10 during business hours.

• • • • • • • • • • • • • • • •

July 19

9:42 a.m. Deputies were called to a report of a rooster in the 39600 block of Amethyst Drive. The rooster was taken to the Steamboat Springs Animal Shelter.

8:08 p.m. Division of Wildlife officers were called to an issue with a porcupine in the 100 block of West Williams Drive in Oak Creek.

69

July 20

11:19 a.m. Police were called to a report of a suspicious incident in the first block of Anglers Court. A woman reported that during the night somebody apparently took the skirting off the backside of her mobile home and turned the lights on in her unlocked car. Nothing was reported stolen.

• • • • • • • • • • • • • • •

July 21

5:12 p.m. Police and deputies were called to help two door-to-door salespeople stranded in Steamboat Springs. The salespeople reported that they had an argument with their boss, and the boss left them in town when he returned to Denver. Police helped the people find a hotel room for the night.

8:27 p.m. Police were called to a complaint about dogs at Whiskey Park in North Routt County. A woman reported that 25 dogs tried to attack her 16-year-old son while they were camping during the weekend. Deputies repeatedly tried to call the woman back but could not reach anybody.

• • • • • • • • • • • • • • •

July 23

8:01 a.m. Police were called to a complaint about juveniles ringing church bells at Seventh and Oak streets.

• • • • • • • • • • • • • • •

July 24

7:14 p.m. Police were called to a disturbance in the 800 block of Howelsen Parkway. A person was arguing with an umpire during a softball game. Everything was fine.

8:08 p.m. Police were called to a request for an officer in the first block of Seventh Street. A woman was taking pictures in the nude. Officers were unable to locate her.

July 27

12:33 a.m. Steamboat Springs Police Department officers were called to a report of vandalism at Village Drive and Walton Creek Road. Two intoxicated men reportedly ripped up flowers but were gone when officers arrived.

10:01 p.m. Police were called to a complaint about a man who reportedly regularly stands on his deck and shouts obscenities in the 300 block of Apple Drive. Officers warned the man.

• • • • • • • • • • • • • • •

July 29

2:04 a.m. Police were called to a report of a disturbance at Village and Medicine Springs drives, where a person reported that two men were fighting. Officers talked to the men and determined they were playing. Everything was fine.

• • • • • • • • • • • • • • •

Aug. 2

8:08 a.m. Deputies were called to a report of two sets of elk horns stolen from a horse trailer in North Routt County sometime during the past week and a half.

1:00 p.m. Police were called to a report of a suspicious order for $170 worth of chicken enchiladas at a business in the 1100 block of Lincoln Avenue. Business owners suspected the order was fraudulent.

• • • • • • • • • • • • • • •

Aug. 10

9:49 p.m. Police were called to a report of a suspicious incident on the Yampa River Core Trail near Fetcher Park. A man reportedly rode his bicycle along the trail, stopped, exposed himself to a woman and rode away.

Aug. 31

2:30 p.m. Police were called to a report of a lost dog at Yampa Valley Medical Center. The 3-pound Chihuahua was found 11 minutes later.

· · · · · · · · · · · · · · · ·

Sept. 2

9:20 p.m. Police were called to a report of two people twirling fire batons in a parking lot in the 2400 block of Pine Grove Road.

· · · · · · · · · · · · · · · ·

Sept. 3

9:58 a.m. Police were called to Yampa Valley Medical Center because a woman had been asking to view newborn babies without the mothers' permission the day before. No contact was made with the woman.

· · · · · · · · · · · · · · · ·

Sept. 6

7:25 a.m. Police were called to a request for an officer at Seventh and Pine streets, where a woman reportedly ignored community safety officers and drove onto a street that was closed for a bicycle race. Officers gave the woman a ticket.

3:07 p.m. Police and Colorado Division of Wildlife officers were called to a report of wildlife in Yampa River Botanic Park. The caller reported being possibly stalked by a large animal. Officers talked to people in the area and walked through the grounds but found no indication of any animal being in the park.

· · · · · · · · · · · · · · · ·

Sept. 7

9:17 a.m. Colorado Division of Wildlife officers and deputies were called to a report of a bear in a chicken coop in the 41000 block of Routt County Road 36. The bear was gone when deputies arrived.

Sept. 8

10:32 p.m. Police were called to a report about a "creepy" trailer at Missouri Avenue and Grand Street.

· · · · · · · · · · · · · · · ·

Sept. 10

11:55 a.m. Deputies were called to a report of students having a party at lunchtime on Boulder Ridge Road. The call was unfounded.

· · · · · · · · · · · · · · · ·

Sept. 15

11:16 a.m. Police were called to a report of a burglary in the 3300 block of Columbine Drive. A man reported that his bong and medical marijuana were missing and he thought he remembered someone being in his bedroom the night before.

· · · · · · · · · · · · · · · ·

Sept. 17

10:02 a.m. Routt County Sheriff's Office deputies were called to a report of a suspicious incident on Coyote Run Court in Oak Creek. A person dialed a wrong number when asking for help with an alpaca that was not feeling well. The person who answered the call was concerned it was a person who was in trouble and called the police. No more information on the alpaca's condition was available.

Sept. 19

10:25 p.m. Police were called to a request to help a person at Ninth Street and Lincoln Avenue. An intoxicated man asked officers to hold his car keys for the night.

• • • • • • • • • • • • • • • •

Sept. 21

3:49 p.m. Deputies were called to a report of a person who threw a lit cigarette butt out of a car window. Officers gave the person a ticket.

• • • • • • • • • • • • • • • •

Sept. 27

1:30 a.m. Police were called to a noise complaint on Mount Village Circle, where two men and a woman reportedly were climbing a tree and being noisy.

• • • • • • • • • • • • • • • •

Oct. 4

6:39 p.m. Police were called to a request for an officer at Stehley Park in the 500 block of North Park Road. The head of a dinosaur statue was reportedly missing.

• • • • • • • • • • • • • • • •

Oct. 6

8:48 a.m. Police were called to a report of men cutting down trees in Little Toots Park in the first block of 12th Street. Officers determined it was city workers in a city truck.

9:49 a.m. A woman made a report at the police station that her neighbor was stealing clothes from inside her house.

• • • • • • • • • • • • • • • •

Oct. 12

3:01 p.m. Routt County sheriff candidate Garrett Wiggins reported that between 50 and 100 of his campaign signs were stolen from across town.

Oct. 6

8:45 a.m. Police and Steamboat Springs Fire Rescue emergency responders were called to a request for help at Soda Creek Elementary School in the 200 block of Park Avenue. A young boy reportedly was stuck inside a foam exercise equipment tube, and emergency responders had to cut him free. The boy was not injured.

Oct. 15

11:56 a.m. Police responded to the 100 block of Anglers Drive, where someone reported they had received flowers from a person they did not want to be in contact with. Officers warned that person to cease contact.

• • • • • • • • • • • • • • • •

Oct. 16

9:53 p.m. Steamboat police were called to reports of a suspicious person in the 2000 block of Curve Plaza. They issued a warning to four people who were selling perfume.

• • • • • • • • • • • • • • • •

Oct. 18

11:16 a.m. Police were called to a report of a theft of the head of a metal sculpture from a park in the 500 block of North Park Road. The head recently was stolen but was reattached and is missing again. The sculpture head is valued at $500.

Oct. 20

5:01 p.m. Police were called to a complaint about a car in the 2500 block of Pine Grove Road. A person reportedly wrapped a chain around a light pole and his car and was driving the car. The caller said the driver appeared to be trying to straighten his bumper or chassis. The driver was gone when officers arrived.

. . . .

Oct. 22

8:38 a.m. Police and Division of Wildlife officers were called to a report of a bear at Starbucks in the 200 block of Anglers Drive. Officers reported the bear had settled down.

. . . .

Oct. 24

10:37 a.m. Steamboat Springs Police Department officers were called to a report of a suspicious incident in the 32000 block of South Lincoln Avenue. A man staying at a hotel reportedly walked out of his shower naked, and a passerby saw him. The man reportedly didn't realize the curtains to his room were open. Officers gave him a warning.

. . . .

Oct. 25

12:16 p.m. Police were called to a report of a theft at the Steamboat Springs High School in the first block of East Maple Street. Somebody reportedly stole a cookie from the cafeteria.

. . . .

Nov. 3

5:13 a.m. Police were called to a report of shots fired in the 300 block of Sixth Street. Officers found a man who had thrown his laptop down the stairs on his deck and reportedly fired a shotgun into the air. Officers arrested a 37-year-old Steamboat man on suspicion of prohibited use of a weapon and disorderly conduct.

Nov. 9

12:13 p.m. Police were called to a report of fraud in the 3300 block of Covey Circle. A person reported that someone called to say the person had won a $350,000 gift card to Walmart but first needed to send money to get the gift. The person did not send any money.

. . . .

Nov. 16

8:35 a.m. Police were called to a report of people selling ornaments in the Central Park Plaza parking lot.

. . . .

Nov. 18

12:28 p.m. Police were called to a report of drugs in the 1900 block of Steamboat Boulevard. A man working in a crawlspace under a building said he found a bench, folding chairs and paint cans with no labels, and he was concerned it was a methamphetamine lab. Officers checked, and everything was fine.

. . . .

Nov. 21

2:54 p.m. Police were called to a report of 15 people sledding on the ski jump in the 800 block of Howelsen Parkway. Officers issued a warning.

Nov. 22

12:23 a.m. Steamboat Springs Police Department officers were called to help a man in the first block of Seventh Street. The man reportedly was kicked out of a bar but his jacket still was inside.

11:08 a.m. Police were called to the 900 block of Pine Grove Circle. A person reportedly was having trouble getting a 3-year-old into a car seat because the child was having a tantrum.

. . . .

Dec. 1

9:09 a.m. Police were called to a report of a theft in the 2300 block of Ski Trail Lane. Somebody reportedly cut down an evergreen tree from a yard, apparently to use as a Christmas tree. There are no suspects.

. . . .

Dec. 8

11:52 p.m. A woman in the 1900 block of Rockies Way was sick and concerned about carbon monoxide after a man repairing her fireplace left to get a part. Firefighters did not find elevated levels of carbon monoxide.

. . . .

Dec. 10

6:51 a.m. Police were called to a request for an officer in the first block of 12th Street. They assisted a person who was locked in the bathroom at Little Toots Park.

. . . .

Dec. 12

7:48 a.m. A Steamboat Springs Transit driver reported seeing someone at a bus stop who looked like a wanted man he or she had seen on TV. Officers were unable to find the person.

Dec. 14

3:40 p.m. A brown rabbit was found in Hillside Village. The incident was referred to animal control officers.

. . . .

Dec. 22

4:26 p.m. A man reported seeing two dogs with porcupine quills in their mouths in the 600 block of Huckleberry Lane. The dogs were taken to a veterinarian.

8:17 p.m. Police issued a warning after seeing people sledding on Ski Trail Lane. A snowball reportedly was thrown at an officer.

. . . .

Dec. 23

8:53 p.m. Police were called to reports of a man at a business in the 1800 block of Central Park Drive banging on and swearing at an ATM because the machine took his card. The man apologized to the manager and left.

. . . .

Dec. 27

1:46 a.m. Police were called to a suspicious incident at Seventh and Yampa streets. Officers issued citations to two women for urinating in public.

9:36 p.m. Police were called to an animal complaint in the 500 block of Lincoln Avenue. A person reported that a black Labrador had icicles on its nose after being outside for a couple of hours while its owner was inside a bar. Police didn't know if officers contacted the owner.

2011

Aug. 24

5:48 a.m. Officers were called to a report of someone "being harassed by rednecks" at a campground in the 3600 block of Lincoln Avenue.

Jan. 5

1:22 p.m. Police issued summonses to two men in the 2300 block of Mount Werner Circle for theft. Police said the men were trying to clip off people's ski lift tickets.

. . . .

Jan. 6

12:04 a.m. Steamboat Springs Police Department officers responded to the 1800 block of Ski Time Square Drive for a report of people fighting at a bar. There were several fights but no known injuries. The bar closed.

. . . .

Jan. 9

4:57 p.m. Police responded to a report of an intoxicated pedestrian at Waterstone Lane and Cascade Drive. Police could not find the man who was reportedly wearing cowboy boots, jeans and a short-sleeved, red-checkered shirt.

. . . .

Jan. 17

10:27 a.m. A person reported finding an elk head on the road.

. . . .

Jan. 26

7:39 a.m. Police were called to a report of two huge elk next to a child drop-off area in the 2800 block of Village Drive.

. . . .

Feb. 6

1:48 a.m. Police were called to a suspicious incident at Seventh Street and Lincoln Avenue. Officers issued a warning to a man who tried to bring an orange construction cone onto a bus. The man returned the cone.

8:19 p.m. Police were called to a report of a suspicious person in the 2300 block of Mount Werner Circle. Officers couldn't find a person who reportedly ripped down signs and Christmas lights.

Jan. 28

4:59 p.m. Police were called to a report of naked people in a hot tub who weren't guests at a condo complex in the 3500 block of Clubhouse Drive. The naked people were gone when officers arrived.

Feb. 9

12:45 p.m. Deputies reported witnessing an inmate at the Routt County Jail throw a lunch plate at a jailer.

. . . .

Feb. 10

1:05 a.m. Routt County Sheriff's Office deputies were called to a report of people arguing over music being played on a karaoke machine in the 60000 block of Routt County Road 129 in Hahn's Peak.

. . . .

Feb. 15

8:58 a.m. Officers were called to a report of a woman who said someone was opening and closing her garage door in the 1800 block of Bear Drive. Police said the woman was having problems operating her garage door.

. . . .

Feb. 17

12:35 a.m. Steamboat Springs Police Department officers witnessed a car accidentally hit an owl at Ninth Street and Lincoln Avenue. The owl died.

Feb. 21

6:27 p.m. Officers were called to a report of a burglary in the 3100 block of Columbine Drive. Underwear was the only thing reported stolen. There are no suspects.

· · · · · · · · · · · · · · · ·

Feb. 27

1:28 p.m. Police were dispatched to a wildlife call in the 1400 block of Steamboat Boulevard. Officers issued a verbal warning to a man who was trying to hand-feed a moose.

· · · · · · · · · · · · · · · ·

March 1

2:08 a.m. Officers were called to a report of a moose blocking a person's front door in the 400 block of Ore House Plaza. The moose moved.

· · · · · · · · · · · · · · · ·

March 3

4:39 p.m. Officers were called to a report of a person getting hit by a snowball in the 1800 block of Ski Time Square Drive. The person was not hurt, and officers were unable to locate the teenagers suspected of throwing the snowball.

· · · · · · · · · · · · · · · ·

March 8

1:52 a.m. Officers were called to a report of a man driving a taxi without a taxi license. Officers contacted the driver, who had a license.

March 11

1:36 a.m. Steamboat Springs Police Department officers were called to the 600 block of Lincoln Avenue, where officers issued two summonses for public indecency to a couple having sex in an alleyway.

9:42 a.m. Police were called to Mountain Village Circle to a report of a wooden object that reportedly fell from the sky and broke someone's window.

· · · · · · · · · · · · · · · ·

March 13

10:50 a.m. Police officers were asked to make an extra patrol in the 200 block of Howelsen Parkway. Police said the patrol was requested during a weekend hockey tournament to ensure safety and "keep the action on the ice."

8:15 p.m. Police were called to a report of a suspicious car in the 2700 block of Laurel Lane. Police said a man and a woman were "messing around" in a car.

10:29 p.m. Police were called to a report of a suspicious person in the 1900 block of Rockies Way. Police said at least one person was highly intoxicated and "running up and down the halls" of a condominium building. Police contacted one person and took him to detox to sober up after he put his pants back on.

March 13

7:08 p.m. Deputies were called to a complaint about a pig loose on Colorado Highway 131 south of Steamboat Springs. Sheriff's Office staff said the pig was on the road and was returned to its pen.

March 15

1:35 a.m. Steamboat Springs Police Department officers were called to a report of girls running on the Steamboat Springs High School football field with glow sticks. Officers asked the girls to leave.

2:41 a.m. Officers were called to a report of a large group of people singing and yelling in the 700 block of Walton Pond Circle.

. . . .

March 18

1:15 p.m. Police were called to a welfare check in the first block of Anglers Drive. An elderly lady told police she presses her Lifeline button about once a month just to make sure it is working.

2:52 p.m. Police were called to a civil complaint in the 2700 block of Crosstimbers Trail, where a construction worker said someone had driven over a roll of brand new carpet the workers had rolled out in a driveway in preparation to install it.

March 20

1:19 p.m. Police were called to help a person in the 300 block of Lincoln Avenue. A 50-year-old woman got her knuckles stuck under the seat of her pickup truck. She called back five minutes later and told police she got her hand free and wouldn't need medical attention.

March 26

3:35 p.m. Police were called to a complaint that teens had bad driving habits at Fourth and Pine streets.

. . . .

March 29

5:29 a.m. Steamboat Springs Police Department officers were called to a report of a man who was annoyed by the backing alarm on a snowplow. Officers could not find the plow.

. . . .

April 4

5:14 p.m. Officers were called to a report of a woman who found a wallet in a ditch while walking five dogs at Mariah Court and Chinook Lane.

. . . .

April 10

12:44 a.m. Police were called to a report of about 10 juveniles estimated to be 10 and 11 years old smoking cigarettes in the 1500 block of Lincoln Avenue. No other information was available.

. . . .

April 11

3:34 p.m. Officers were called to a report of a man screaming, yelling obscenities and crying from a balcony at Seventh and Oak streets.

. . . .

April 14

7:38 a.m. Officers were called to a report of a man who ordered a gaming system online and received a pair of headphones instead.

. . . .

April 21

7:39 p.m. Officers issued a summons to a man for stealing a bottle of garlic powder from a grocery store in the 1800 block of Central Park Drive.

April 26

11:23 a.m. Officers were called to a report of a woman having trouble with a taxidermist in the 2300 block of Lincoln Avenue. The woman got an animal mounted and paid for it with jewelry. She wanted to return the mount, but the taxidermist did not want to return the jewelry. Officers told the people it was a civil situation that would need to be settled in court.

. . . .

April 27

2:42 p.m. Officers were called to a report of a man who found a bullet hole in a wall of the condo he was looking after in the 1300 block of Skyview Lane. A man in the neighboring condo had accidentally fired a gun that he was cleaning and thought was unloaded.

. . . .

April 28

12:22 p.m. Officers were called to a report of a man and woman panhandling with a puppy at Central Park Drive and Pine Grove Road. They were given a warning.

. . . .

April 30

3:09 p.m. Police were called to a report of shots fired on Anglers Drive. Police said the report was unfounded. Police said young teenagers in Fish Creek Mobile Home Park were using candy to increase pressure inside a plastic soda bottle, causing the bottle to expand and burst. Police issued a warning and talked to the teens' parents.

April 28 — **3:04 a.m.** Steamboat Springs Police Department officers were called to a report of a bear that went through an electric fence and killed eight chickens in the 700 block of Princeton Avenue. Officers chased the bear away.

May 3

6:35 p.m. Officers were called to a report of a drunken man climbing a tree in front of a business at Ninth Street and Lincoln Avenue.

. . . .

May 4

10:49 a.m. Deputies were called to a report of kids riding in a car without seat belts near mile marker 127 on U.S. Highway 40.

. . . .

May 5

12:19 p.m. Officers were called about a group of juveniles boxing at Howelsen Hill. They were told to stop.

. . . .

May 8

4:59 p.m. Police responded to a complaint about a car on Howelsen Parkway. Police said a city employee complained about a car "pond-skimming" on the road, which was covered in floodwater from the Yampa River.

. . . .

May 11

5:55 p.m. Officers were called to a report of a scruffy man in his 30s handing out cards for low-cost prescription drugs at the downtown post office.

May 13

12:24 p.m. Officers were called to the 600 block of Lincoln Avenue by a man who reported his backpack was stolen the night before. Officers later found the backpack in one of four cars that were burglarized in Dream Island Plaza. He was booked into Routt County Jail on suspicion of first-degree trespassing, theft and false reporting.

May 23

12:20 p.m. Officers were called to a report of a woman who had cut cables coming from a utility box in the first block of Butcherknife Alley. Police say the woman was upset because the utility company had not repaired the box, which was damaged and had a garbage bag over it. Police helped mediate the situation and allowed the utility company to work the situation out with the woman.

May 24

11:37 p.m. Officers were called to a report of a disturbance between neighbors in the 200 block of Blue Sage Circle. A man reported that his puppy had chewed up the inside of his car, and he was yelling at his dog when his neighbor confronted him about the way he was treating his dog.

June 1

7:25 a.m. Steamboat Springs Police Department officers were called to a report of a one-way sign that had been vandalized to say "stoner way" at Ninth and Pine streets.

June 1

12:20 p.m. Officers helped Steamboat Springs Fire Rescue emergency responders with a report of strange smells at a condo in the 1800 block of Loggers Lane. The smell went away.

8:09 p.m. Officers were called to a report of two bears on the deck of a home and a woman inside who was "freaking out" in the 1900 block of Fish Creek Falls Road. The bears did not enter the home and were scared away.

June 3

10:39 p.m. Police were contacted by two people at Yampa and Seventh streets who asked if two margaritas were enough to get them drunk.

April 18

2:06 p.m. Officers were called to a report of a woman in the 2200 block of Après Ski Way who reported that a cargo container was missing from the top of her car. The woman later found the container at the car wash she had driven through earlier.

June 3

10:55 p.m. Deputies and U.S. Forest Service officers were called to a report of several cars passing through locked Forest Service road gates in North Routt County. Law enforcement officers found a large group of high school students camping in the area, and the Forest Service issued 50 to 55 citations for operating motor vehicles on a closed Forest Service road.

• • • • • • • • • • • • • • • •

June 4

12:06 a.m. Steamboat Springs Police Department officers were called to a report of a suspicious incident in the 600 block of Yampa Street. A man was kicking a longboard skateboard into the street in front of cars.

• • • • • • • • • • • • • • • •

June 6

3:57 p.m. Officers were called to a report of a woman stealing hot dogs and other items from a grocery store in the 1800 block of Central Park Drive. The woman was arrested on an outstanding warrant.

• • • • • • • • • • • • • • • •

June 7

7:06 p.m. Officers were called to a report of people who were upset because they were putting sandbags in a place that the property manager did not think was appropriate at Dream Island Mobile Home Park.

• • • • • • • • • • • • • • • •

June 9

12:36 a.m. Officers were called to a report of a noise complaint in the 2900 block of Columbine Drive. A person was "screaming their head off," and police gave a warning.

10:57 p.m. Officers were called to a report of a group of people "hooting and hollering" at the top of Laurel Lane.

June 13

12:44 p.m. Hayden Police Department officers were called to a juvenile situation. Two girls, ages 5 and 7, had a disagreement about a lunchbox.

10:51 p.m. Police were called to a juvenile situation in the 200 block of Park Avenue. A person thought a group of juveniles was smoking marijuana because they were coughing. Offices contacted the juveniles, who were playing Frisbee, and asked them to leave.

• • • • • • • • • • • • • • • •

June 19

10:44 p.m. Police and Division of Wildlife officers were called to a report of a bear in the 300 block of Pearl Street. Callers reported that a bear was getting into a trash can and chewing on a grill before knocking it over. The bear was gone when officers arrived.

• • • • • • • • • • • • • • • •

June 21

8:26 p.m. Officers were called to Centennial Hall for a report of people having a "heated debate" about medical marijuana.

• • • • • • • • • • • • • • • •

June 24

9:36 a.m. Police and Steamboat Springs Fire Rescue emergency responders were called to a report of smoke in the 800 block of Lincoln Avenue. Someone had left a curling iron on a piece of plastic, and it began smoking. There was no fire.

10:44 a.m. Officers helped Colorado Division of Wildlife officers with a bear cub that was stranded on an island in the Yampa River near the first block of Anglers Drive. Officers helped reunite the cub with its mother.

May 29

June 26

12:39 p.m. Police were called to a report of a stolen car in the 400 block of Eighth Street. The owner reported leaving the car parked overnight with the keys in the ignition but couldn't find it in the morning. Officers found the car at Eighth and Oak streets with the keys still in the ignition.

2:56 p.m. Police were called to a report of shoplifting in the 1800 block of Central Park Drive. A woman tried to push a full grocery cart out of the store without paying. Officers issued her a summons to appear in court.

. . . .

June 27

9:13 p.m. Officers were called to a report of a man interfering with road striping and taunting workers in Central Park Plaza. They warned the man.

July 4

2:03 a.m. Steamboat Springs Police Department officers were called to a report of a person ringing a doorbell and leaving in the 300 block of Lincoln Avenue.

. . . .

July 5

12:36 a.m. Officers were called to a report of a man smoking marijuana in back of a bar in the 600 block of Yampa Street. The man tried to punch an employee after the employee approached him. The man ran away, and police did not find him.

. . . .

July 14

12:09 p.m. Officers were called to a report of a woman who lost her cellphone while partying the previous evening in the mountain area.

. . . .

July 15

7:06 a.m. Someone dropped off a baby duck in a box at the police station, and Animal Control took it to the shelter. The baby duck is fine.

5:11 p.m. Police were called to a report of someone putting a giant rope out in the street to act as a speed bump in the 1000 block of Crawford Avenue. Officers removed the rope. Three hours later, people put the rope out again. Officers removed the rope a second time and issued a warning.

. . . .

July 16

5:34 p.m. Officers were called to a report of a suspicious incident at 11th Street and Crawford Avenue. A person called police saying a neighbor was putting debris in the road to slow down traffic. The neighbors were told by police to stop putting debris in the road.

July 16

6:29 p.m. Officers were called to a report of a disturbance in the first block of Maple Street. Officers mediated a verbal argument between a coach and a referee at a soccer game.

. . . .

July 19

5:04 p.m. Officers were called to a report of a sick and pregnant woman who had gotten off a Greyhound bus to use the bathroom at Stock Bridge Transit Center, and the bus left without her. The bus returned to get the woman.

. . . .

July 22

9:48 p.m. Police were called to a report of a car driving on the Yampa River Core Trail near Stock Bridge Transit Center. The car was driving on the trail by mistake.

. . . .

July 24

2:01 p.m. Police were called to a report that two boys were planting something that looked like marijuana in the first block of Anglers Drive. No other information was available.

July 25

4:16 a.m. Steamboat Springs Police Department officers were called to a report of a bear in a garage in the 300 block of Blue Sage Circle. The bear had forced its way out of a metal door by the time officers arrived.

5:05 p.m. Officers were called to a report of juveniles throwing water balloons from a cliff above the Yampa River near 13th Street.

. . . .

July 26

10:14 p.m. Steamboat officers were called to a report of a "seriously large bear" that had flipped over a trash can and hit a car with it in the first block of Anglers Drive.

July 13

10:26 a.m. Officers were called to a report of a car that drove through the window of a restaurant at Fourth Street and Lincoln Avenue. The car hit two other cars before crashing, but no one was seriously hurt. Police issued a careless driving ticket to the driver of the car that went into the restaurant.

July 29

2:09 a.m. Police were called to a report of an intoxicated woman on Cypress Court. She told officers she would "stumble home."

8:38 p.m. Police and deputies were called to a report of a person who had broken into a car in the 400 block of Lincoln Avenue. Officers found a 27-year-old Steamboat Springs man inside the car, pouring alcohol on the three dogs that had been left there. He was arrested on suspicion of first-degree criminal trespass, second-degree criminal tampering and possession of marijuana.

· · · · · · · · · · · · · · · ·

July 31

4:42 a.m. Officers were called to a report of a suspicious person on the Yampa River Core Trail. A man in his 20s threw a backpack into the river and ran away when he saw officers approaching. Police were unable to find the backpack or the man who threw it.

· · · · · · · · · · · · · · · ·

Aug. 3

7:41 a.m. Officers were called to a report of a naked woman running down the street and dancing at Riverside Drive and U.S. Highway 40. The woman was taken into custody and transported to Yampa Valley Medical Center.

Aug. 5

11:05 a.m. Deputies were called to a report of a theft of a traffic counter on Routt County Road 5 near Toponas. The Routt County Road and Bridge Department was using the device to monitor traffic.

· · · · · · · · · · · · · · · ·

Aug. 6

9:27 a.m. Officers were called to inspect a grenade in the 800 block of Pahwintah Street. Police said the owner of the grenade wanted to verify it wasn't live. Officers determined it was a dud.

· · · · · · · · · · · · · · · ·

Aug. 7

12:41 a.m. Officers were called to a complaint of "bad '80s karaoke" music in the 300 block of Crabapple Court.

2:03 a.m. Officers were called to a report of a man on a horse lassoing objects in the 400 block of Howelsen Parkway.

7:29 p.m. Officers were called to a report of a person squirting an unidentified white liquid on a playground in the 200 block of Park Avenue. Police suspect it was sunscreen.

Sept. 10

8:54 p.m. Officers were called to a report of a burglary in the first block of West Acres Drive. Police arrested a 57-year-old woman on suspicion of second-degree burglary after officers said the woman stole an unknown amount of money from the home. She was caught after the homeowners found her cane inside the home and were able to trace it back to her.

7:44 p.m. Officers were called to a report of a disturbance in the 2600 block of Longthong Court. Officers found a group of men participating in what police called a competitive game of dominoes.

July 26

Aug. 8

1:38 a.m. Steamboat Springs Police Department officers were called to a report of "a couple guys raising a ruckus" at a bar in the 700 block of Yampa Street. The men were asked to leave.

9:25 p.m. Deputies were called to a report of gunshots in the 400 block of Meadowbrook Court in Hayden. The noise came from a video game.

· · · · · · · · · · · · · · · ·

Aug. 14

2:18 p.m. Police were called to an animal complaint at Whistler and Walton Creek roads. An injured bird in a box was given to an officer, who took it to a veterinarian.

· · · · · · · · · · · · · · · ·

Aug. 18

12:12 a.m. Steamboat Springs Police Department officers were called to a report of men talking about explosives at a bar in the 600 block of Lincoln Avenue.

Aug. 19

11:14 p.m. Police were called to a report of a fight in the 3100 block of South Lincoln Avenue. A man who had been kicked out of a bar returned and punched a bartender in the face. The bartender did not press charges.

· · · · · · · · · · · · · · · ·

Aug. 21

3:47 p.m. Police were called to a report that juveniles were using their bikes to jump off the handicap ramp at Fetcher Park. Officers asked them to stop.

· · · · · · · · · · · · · · · ·

Aug. 24

2:19 p.m. Officers were called to a report of a man taking pictures of a woman and her daughter in Steamboat. The man told the woman he was an artist, and he left.

· · · · · · · · · · · · · · · ·

Sept. 5

9:13 p.m. Officers were called to a report of a woman whose roommate moved out but did not take her bed. She left it at the end of the driveway in the 1000 block of 13th Street.

Sept. 23

9:50 p.m. Police were called to a noise complaint in the 800 block of Howelsen Parkway because of a kickball tournament. Officers told the participants to quiet down.

11:50 p.m. Police were called to a report of vandalism at Lincoln Avenue and Seventh Street, where someone reportedly had kicked in the glass of a bus shelter. The suspect had blue face paint and was wearing a cape.

Sept. 7

6:23 a.m. Steamboat Springs Police Department officers were called to a report of a bear that chased after a woman's boyfriend in the 500 block of Pine Street. The woman thought it was because the bear was protecting its cubs. The bear was chased up a tree.

· · · · · · · · · · · · · · · ·

Sept. 9

1:21 a.m. Steamboat Springs Police Department officers were called to a report of a woman sleeping in her car at Seventh and Yampa streets. Officers warned the woman and then warned her again 30 minutes later when she hadn't left.

· · · · · · · · · · · · · · · ·

Sept. 21

10:19 p.m. Deputies were called to a report of multiple people walking around with flashlights at the Oak Creek Cemetery.

· · · · · · · · · · · · · · · ·

Sept. 22

5:41 a.m. Officers were called to a report of a woman who said that there was a fox near her car and that she was afraid to get into her car in the 900 block of Lincoln Avenue. The fox could not be found.

Nov. 22

6:53 p.m. Officers were called to a report of a suspicious incident at a resort in the 2800 block of Village Drive. A security guard reported seeing a man with a shaved head who had locked himself in a storage shed and was wearing a trash bag. The man changed clothes and then walked toward the pool area. The man was contacted, and he was an employee at the resort. Everything was fine.

Sept. 26

4:29 p.m. Firefighters were called to a report of a car that drove off U.S. Highway 40 about one mile east of Hayden. A bee had gotten into a woman's car, and she drove off the road while trying to fight the bee. The woman was not hurt, and the car was not severely damaged except for flat tires.

6:28 p.m. Officers were called to a report of a woman who was highly intoxicated in the 700 block of Oak Street. Officers contacted the 44-year-old woman, who told officers she had been dropped off downtown and she was supposed to meet a man who was at an Alcoholics Anonymous meeting.

· · · · · · · · · · · · · · · ·

Oct. 2

10:19 a.m. Officers were called to a report of a suspicious incident in the 3100 block of Ingles Lane. A man called police to say a pop-up advertisement on his Internet browser was asking for his credit card number. Police advised the man not to enter his credit card number.

· · · · · · · · · · · · · · · ·

Oct. 6

12:06 p.m. Officers were called to a report of fraud in the 400 block of Anglers Drive. A person received a phone call from someone who said if he or she sent $750, he or she would receive $3.5 million.

· · · · · · · · · · · · · · · ·

Oct. 14

6:22 a.m. Police were called to the 600 block of Marketplace Plaza to a report of a suspicious person in a vehicle who a business owner thought was stealing wireless Internet. The person actually was reading a newspaper.

Dec. 23

3:04 a.m. Deputies were called to a report of a man displaying odd behavior at a gas station on Colorado Highway 131 in Yampa. The man reportedly was wrestling and fighting with a trash can. Deputies contacted the man, and he was fine.

Oct. 23

6:11 p.m. Officers were called to a report of a suspicious person in the 1800 block of Central Park Drive. A Steamboat man told police that at about 7 a.m., he saw a man with a shaved head in the grocery store who looked like a crime suspect whose sketch was shown on 9News.

· · · · · · · · · · · · · · · ·

Nov. 16

11:56 a.m. Officers were called to a report of a disturbance at a doctor's office on Pine Grove Road. A husband reportedly threw divorce papers at his wife's face.

11:24 p.m. Officers were called to a report of a suspicious person in the 500 block of Marketplace Plaza. A man reportedly had walked up and down all the shopping aisles in the convenience store and had been in the restroom for 20 minutes. The man left, and police were unable to find him.

Nov. 29

1:12 p.m. Officers were called to a report of a person complaining about a driver who honks the horn of a car every morning in the 1300 block of Athens Plaza.

• • • • • • • • • • • • • • • •

Dec. 1

3:44 a.m. Officers were called to a report of noise in the 400 block of Gilpin Street. A person reportedly was making a 10-foot-tall sculpture in his or her yard.

• • • • • • • • • • • • • • • •

Dec. 3

8:56 p.m. Officers were called to a report of a theft in the 300 block of Third Street. Police said hundreds of dollars worth of firewood was reported stolen out of a residence.

Dec. 16

5:10 p.m. Officers and Steamboat Springs Fire Rescue responded to a report of a disturbance in the 3700 block of Lincoln Avenue. Two brothers had gotten into a fight, and one had hit the other in the head with a frying pan. The brother with the frying pan fled the scene. The injured man was treated on scene and did not want to press charges.

• • • • • • • • • • • • • • • •

Dec. 22

12:30 a.m. Steamboat Springs Police Department officers were called to a report of a large snowball fight involving about 15 men at Steamboat Ski Area. Officers showed up and determined that no laws were being broken.

Dec. 11

9:21 p.m. Officers and deputies were called to a report of a fight in the 600 block of Lincoln Avenue. Officers later arrested a 44-year-old Steamboat man on suspicion of harassment, disorderly conduct, obstructing a police officer and resisting arrest after he was found on horseback near the Depot Art Center. Police said they had to use a Taser on the man after he repeatedly ignored commands from the arresting officers. During the night, the man and his two friends had gone into a grocery store and local watering holes on horseback.

· · · · · · · · 2012 · · · · · · · ·

May 8

8:34 a.m. Deputies were called to a report of fraud in the 14000 block of Routt County Road 7 near Yampa. A man reported purchasing a donkey from a person on Craigslist, and the man was upset because he thought the Craigslist description was not an accurate representation of the donkey. Deputies referred the man to the civil courts.

Jan. 1

9:26 a.m. Officers were called to a report of a burglary in the 2200 block of Storm Meadows Drive. The manager of a laundry facility thought someone took money from a laundry machine that should have contained a couple hundred dollars. The laundry manager discovered the machine was not taking money properly.

• • • • • • • • • • • • • • •

Jan. 6

8:52 a.m. Routt County Sheriff's Office deputies were called to a report of a stolen vehicle in the 27000 block of Aspen Valley Lane. A 38-year-old Steamboat Springs man had reported his motorcycle stolen to a Texas police department, but deputies found that he had been hiding it, and the man was arrested for false reporting and felony criminal attempted theft.

• • • • • • • • • • • • • • •

Jan. 12

12:26 p.m. Officers were called to a report of a person who thought a footprint in the snow looked weird in the 1500 block of Shadow Run Frontage. Everything was fine.

Jan. 5

11:14 p.m. Officers were called to a report of vandalism in the 2200 block of Storm Meadows Drive. A person reportedly threw a rock at a pizza delivery car because the pizza delivery person could not find the correct address.

Jan. 12

7:23 p.m. Officers were called to a report of a suspicious person in the 3000 block of Chinook Lane. Officers found a group of juveniles inside a house, but they probably had permission to be there. Officers do not think the juveniles had permission to smoke marijuana in the house, and officers gave a ticket for possession of marijuana.

• • • • • • • • • • • • • • •

Jan. 18

11:26 p.m. Officers were called to a report of a young male in the first block of Anglers Drive who was playing chicken with a train. He could not be found.

• • • • • • • • • • • • • • •

Jan. 23

12:30 a.m. Officers were called to a report of a computer lost at 11th and Oak streets. A person thought it might have fallen off the top of his or her car somewhere downtown.

• • • • • • • • • • • • • • •

Jan. 29

1:27 p.m. Officers, Steamboat Springs Fire Rescue and mental health professionals were called to a suspicious incident in the 41000 block of Routt County Road 129. A man reported that men hiding in trees with weapons were trying to kill him. The man was taken to Yampa Valley Medical Center.

• • • • • • • • • • • • • • •

Feb. 2

9:11 a.m. Officers were called to check on a man who had not shown up for work. The man did not show up for work because he was in jail.

4:50 p.m. Officers were called to a report of a suspicious person at Heavenly View and Steamboat Boulevard. The person was using binoculars to watch moose that were shedding antlers.

5:17 p.m. Police officers and deputies were called to a report of a suspicious-looking item in a yard in the 2400 block of Ski Trail Lane. Police officers investigated the item and determined it was a potato.

Feb. 17

Feb. 5

9:10 p.m. Police arrested a 27-year-old Steamboat man on suspicion of theft, driving under the influence and possession of marijuana after being called to a report that a man was trying to put an entire cart of unbagged groceries in the bed of his truck. An employee confronted the man before he drove away.

. . . .

Feb. 14

1:16 a.m. Officers were called to a report of about 10 kids having fun and making noise in the first block of Cypress Court. Officers gave a warning.

. . . .

Feb. 22

9:37 p.m. Officers were called to a report of a person who lost an earring valued at $7,500 somewhere downtown.

. . . .

Feb. 27

1:28 p.m. Deputies were called to check on the welfare of a person in the first block of Moffat Avenue in Yampa. A friend was concerned about a woman because she recently had lost her job, and the friend had not heard from her. The woman was fine. She was just sleeping in.

March 5

3:26 a.m. Officers were called to a report of a person complaining about noise from snowplows in the 1800 block of Ski Time Square Drive. Snowplows are exempt from the noise ordinance, and the plows were finished plowing when officers arrived.

. . . .

March 7

1:00 p.m. Deputies were called to a report of a suspicious incident in Hayden. A woman said she recently got a new cellphone number and was receiving disturbing text messages related to drugs.

. . . .

March 9

12:16 a.m. Officers were called to a report of a disturbance in the 1600 block of Graystone Drive. Two women were slapping each other, and neither one wanted to press charges.

. . . .

March 10

1:30 a.m. Steamboat Springs Police Department officers and Steamboat Fire Rescue firefighters were called to a report of an assault in the 600 block of Lincoln Avenue. Police said a woman accused a 27-year-old man of touching her butt inappropriately. Police said the woman's boyfriend, a 26-year-old Steamboat man, then punched the man who was accused of touching the woman. Officers arrested the 27-year-old man on suspicion of unlawful sexual contact, and the 26-year-old man was arrested on suspicion of third-degree assault and possession of drug paraphernalia.

10:38 a.m. Officers were called to a report of someone putting trash on a vehicle parked in the 3100 block of Ingles Lane. Police said the trash was a letter complaining about how badly the car was parked.

March 14

5:50 p.m. Officers were called to a report of a drunken driver in the 1400 block of South Lincoln Avenue. A woman called and said she saw a woman pouring beer into a coffee cup while driving. A 43-year-old Milner woman was arrested on suspicion of driving while ability impaired.

• • • • • • • • • • • • • • •

March 22

11:21 a.m. Deputies were called to a report of people skateboarding down Rabbit Ears Pass. They were warned not to.

1:23 p.m. Deputies were called to a report of a drunken driver near Heritage Park on U.S. Highway 40. No alcohol was involved. The elderly driver was given a ticket and a recommendation to take a driving class.

• • • • • • • • • • • • • • •

March 31

5:41 p.m. Officers were called to a report of a suspicious incident in the 200 block of Seventh Street. Police said a man returned home from out of town and found beer cans and a cellphone on his coffee table that didn't belong to him. Upon further investigation, police learned that a highly intoxicated man in his 30s entered the other man's home, which was unlocked, the night before and mistakenly thought it was his own. The intoxicated man then passed out on the couch and left the items behind. The homeowner did not press charges against the man because nothing was damaged or missing.

• • • • • • • • • • • • • • •

April 5

2:13 p.m. Steamboat Springs Police Department officers were called to a report of shoplifting at a grocery store in the 1800 block of Central Park Drive. A 46-year-old man was arrested on suspicion of stealing antifungal cream worth less than $10.

April 8

7:33 a.m. Routt County Sheriff's Office deputies were called to a report of a truck that had been stolen from the 200 block of Carbon Avenue in Oak Creek and taken for a "joyride." The owner of the vehicle told deputies he found cigarette butts in the truck that didn't belong to him, and the truck's gas level was lower. Deputies didn't have any suspects.

• • • • • • • • • • • • • • •

April 12

12:04 p.m. Officers were called to a report of shoplifting at a grocery store in the 1800 block of Central Park Drive. A man was suspected of taking a couple of Bud Light beers and was cited.

• • • • • • • • • • • • • • •

April 13

2:29 p.m. Officers were called to a report of a vehicle parked at a campground with five people in it. Police contacted the people and determined they were just taking pictures.

• • • • • • • • • • • • • • •

April 15

11:20 a.m. Officers were called to a report of a suspicious incident in the 700 block of Critter Court. An employee at Steamboat Springs Animal Shelter reported that the driver of a Honda had been parking outside of the shelter the last four Sundays. Police made contact with the driver and determined he had been parking there to take a nap, and everything was OK.

April 23

11:48 a.m. Officers were called to a report of a suspicious person in the first block of Balsam Court. The caller said the suspicious person didn't look like he or she belonged. Officers did not find the person.

. . . .

April 30

3:38 p.m. Officers were called to a report of marijuana plants found in a Dumpster at Colorado Mountain College. Officers seized the four or five baby plants. The incident is under investigation.

. . . .

May 1

12:44 a.m. Steamboat Springs Police Department officers were called to a report of a bear at Oak and Ninth streets. It was sitting in the middle of the road and was chased away.

. . . .

May 3

10:42 p.m. Deputies were called to a report of a suspicious incident in the 51400 block of Buck Mountain Lane near Steamboat. A woman reported finding strange items in her house, including costume jewelry.

. . . .

May 4

7:00 a.m. Routt County Sheriff's Office deputies were called to a report of a deer that looked exhausted or sick by the road near Mad Creek trailhead on Routt County Road 129. The deer was gone when officers arrived.

2:58 p.m. Deputies were called to help a person who claimed they found a pile of wood that belonged to them on someone else's property. The wood had been missing since October 2011.

2:00 a.m. Steamboat Springs Police Department officers were called to a report of a suspicious incident in the 1300 block of Manitou Avenue. Police said a homeowner reported finding a stranger using a bathroom in the home. The residents chased the person away.

April 21

May 7

11:02 p.m. Officers were called to a report of a person in the 2400 block of Lincoln Avenue who passed a bus stop and saw a man that may have urinated on himself, was acting strange and was jumping in front of traffic. The man left the bus stop.

. . . .

May 9

5:57 p.m. Deputies were called to a report of a woman who thought her ex-husband was sending people to her house to try to sell things in the 32600 block of Colorado Highway 131.

. . . .

May 11

7:40 p.m. Officers were called to a report of a minor trying to get a tattoo using fake identification in the 800 block of Lincoln Avenue.

May 11

10:19 p.m. Officers were called to a report of noise in the 2500 block of Riverside Drive. It was a family hosting a graduation party, and they were asked to be quiet.

. . . .

May 17

9:06 a.m. Officers were called to help a person in the 900 block of Lincoln Avenue. The owner of a car said there was a "woodchuck-looking varmint" under the hood of the car, and she wanted help. An animal control officer was not available to help.

. . . .

May 18

1:02 p.m. Deputies were called to a report of a suspicious incident in the 32700 block of Waters Edge Court near Steamboat. A man thought someone had broken into his house because there was a loaf of bread on the kitchen counter, and he did not know who put it there. The man had last been at the house around Christmas.

May 23

2:58 p.m. Officers were called to a report of a person who was concerned about a bear on Pine Street because children were about to get out of school. Parks and Wildlife officers tranquilized the bear, which then became stuck in the tree. Steamboat Springs Fire Rescue firefighters were called to help get the bear down so it could be relocated outside of Steamboat.

. . . .

May 29

11:34 p.m. Officers were called to a report of four teenage boys running from a parking lot at Steamboat Springs High School toward the Spring Creek Trail. Officers think the teens were planning a senior prank.

. . . .

June 1

11:42 a.m. Colorado Division of Parks and Wildlife officers were called to a report of a baby moose stuck in a barbed-wire fence in the 35700 block of U.S. Highway 40. The moose got out of the fence on its own.

May 12

10:00 a.m. Officers pulled over a vehicle traveling 5 mph that had all of its tires flattened, its roof caved in and windshield busted out. Police said the driver, a 41-year-old Steamboat woman, rolled the vehicle down an embankment near the Steamboat Springs Cemetery and was trying to continue to drive home after suffering minor injuries. The woman was taken to the hospital and arrested on suspicion of driving under the influence of alcohol.

1:52 p.m. Officers were called to a report of a burglary in the 3100 block of Elk River Road. The resident reported someone went inside the home and urinated in a bottle of juice. It was discovered when the resident smelled an odor coming from the juice. Officers were investigating possible suspects.

June 5

June 8

12:56 a.m. Officers were called to a report of a person who had been chased by a bear that was in a Dumpster in the 2500 block of Cattle Kate Circle. The bear could not be found.

12:11 p.m. Routt County Search and Rescue volunteers were called to rescue a 14-year-old boy who was stranded on a rock face at Fish Creek Falls. The boy was able to come down with some help.

. . . .

June 13

2:10 p.m. Officers were called to a report of a man who was being harassed by another man at a gas station in the 2000 block of Curve Plaza. The man told police he was being yelled at because he owns a medical marijuana dispensary.

June 13

2:29 p.m. Officers were called to a report of a suspicious incident in the 900 block of Oak Street. A woman thought someone had been in her home because the toilet seat was up.

. . . .

June 15

5:36 p.m. Deputies were called to a report of a fight at the Routt County Jail. Deputies think the fight between two male inmates started when an inmate took another inmate's plate of food. One inmate had minor injuries, and the other inmate was arrested on suspicion of third-degree assault.

. . . .

June 17

9:11 p.m. Deputies were called to a report of a suspicious incident on Rabbit Ears Pass. A person reported seeing a flashing light. It was a deputy on a traffic stop.

. . . .

June 19

10:20 p.m. Officers were called to a report of a missing person at Mount Werner Road and Montview Lane after a couple had gotten off a bus and the male suddenly couldn't locate his girlfriend. The girlfriend was found at their condo, where they were headed.

. . . .

June 23

10:59 a.m. Officers were called to a report of a burglary in the 2100 block of Mount Werner Circle. Upon further investigation, police determined the owner of the residence locked himself out of his home and kicked in his own door to get back inside.

. . . .

June 28

3:26 p.m. Officers were called to a report of two boys playing with cap guns at Mariah Court and Zephyr Trail. The person who reported it was concerned a spark from the guns could start a fire.

June 28

7:04 p.m. Steamboat Springs Fire Rescue firefighters were called to help with a flower bed that was smoldering in the 1800 block of Central Park Drive.

8:01 p.m. Officers were called to a report of an illegal fire in the 800 block of Weiss Circle. People were grilling cheeseburgers, and everything was fine.

9:06 p.m. Oak Creek Fire Protection District firefighters were called to a report of a structure fire near mile marker 12 on Routt County Road 16. Two sheds were on fire, and 30 turkeys died. The fire was extinguished.

· · · · · · · · · · · · · · ·

June 29

3:54 p.m. Officers were called to a report of two drunken men who were starting to take their clothes off at a bar in the 1800 block of Ski Time Square Drive. One of the men was arrested on an outstanding warrant.

July 1

10:00 a.m. Officers were called to a report of a suspicious incident in the 2900 block of West Acres Drive. A woman told police she found several strange things in her house, including an ash tray, that led her to think someone had been in her home illegally.

· · · · · · · · · · · · · · ·

July 2

9:57 p.m. Police were called to a report of teenagers possibly playing catch with and dropping eggs in the parking lot of a business in the 1100 block of South Lincoln Avenue.

· · · · · · · · · · · · · · ·

July 3

10:45 p.m. Officers were called to a report of a beer tap that had been damaged at a bar in the 700 block of Yampa Street. Surveillance video showed a man reached over and twisted the tap in an attempt to drink beer from it. Officers were following up on the incident.

June 24

6:26 p.m. Officers were called to a report of a drunken woman who was acting strangely outside of a hotel in the 3100 block of U.S. Highway 40. Police said they found the 35-year-old woman laying in the grass trying to hide from police by covering herself with branches. Officers said the woman then lied about who she was. As officers attempted to arrest the woman, she attacked them and screamed threats at them. The woman was arrested on suspicion of second-degree assault, attempting to influence a public servant, resisting arrest and violating multiple protection orders. Officers were not injured.

July 5

11:15 p.m. Officers were called to a report of a burglary at an apartment in the 1300 block of Dream Island Plaza. A computer was taken, and the burglar put a pressurized can of cheese in the microwave and left the microwave on. It did not cause damage, and the incident is under investigation.

. . . .

July 8

8:41 p.m. Deputies were called to a report of a disturbance in the first block of East First Street in Oak Creek. Deputies mediated an argument between a father and son who were fighting about a chain saw.

. . . .

July 9

8:59 a.m. Officers were called to speak with a man who thought his kids were smoking marijuana in his car.

. . . .

July 11

4:51 p.m. Officers were called to a report of a man wearing a cowboy hat who was smoking marijuana outside the Yampa Valley Medical Center emergency room. The man left in a car, and officers could not find him.

. . . .

July 13

12:58 p.m. Officers were called to a report of people throwing rocks onto the road in the 3600 block of Lincoln Avenue. People actually were collecting rocks from the hillside because, apparently, some of them contain crystals.

. . . .

July 16

4:25 p.m. Officers were called to a report of people at a bus stop throwing cigarette butts on the ground at Seventh Street and Lincoln Avenue. The group had gotten on a bus by the time police arrived.

July 27

4:13 p.m. Deputies were called to a report of a suspicious incident in the 36100 block of Routt County Road 51 near Hayden. A man found a rattlesnake in his mailbox, and he thought someone put it there as a prank.

July 23

8:44 a.m. Officers were called to a report of a person who lost his or her wallet. The person thought he or she left it at a lemonade stand on Amethyst Drive.

9:30 p.m. A person turned in a purse found in the Elk River. It appeared the purse had been in the river for about 10 years because the contents were dissolved, rusted or disintegrated.

. . . .

July 25

10:46 a.m. Officers were called to a report of two women who left a restaurant without paying in the 3100 block of South Lincoln Avenue. A 38-year-old Steamboat woman and a 26-year-old Steamboat woman who were celebrating one of their birthdays were arrested on suspicion of theft and taking alcohol from a licensed premise.

. . . .

July 27

10:08 p.m. Officers were called to a report of people throwing snowballs in the 1100 block of South Lincoln Avenue. The person called back to say water balloons were being thrown.

5:41 a.m. Officers were called to a report of a skunk that had a glass bottle stuck on its head in the first block of Anglers Drive. Officers could not find the skunk.

July 3

July 30

9:00 p.m. Officers were called to a report of sprinklers shooting water into the air at Sixth and Pine streets.

• • • • • • • • • • • • • • • •

Aug. 3

3:06 p.m. Deputies were called to a report of a person who threw a wrapper from a car near mile marker 138 on U.S. Highway 40.

• • • • • • • • • • • • • • • •

Aug. 4

10:47 a.m. Officers were called to a report of a suspicious incident downtown. A woman called police and told them she took her car to the mechanic after it was driving funny, and the mechanic told her it likely had loose lug nuts. Police said the woman wanted to let police know "in case it happened to anyone else."

• • • • • • • • • • • • • • • •

Aug. 5

3:01 a.m. Officers were called to a report of a balding older man running around in his boxer shorts at 10th Street and Lincoln Avenue. Police said the man accidentally locked himself out of his nearby hotel room and was trying to get some help getting back in. Police helped the man get back into his room.

Aug. 6

6:41 p.m. Officers were called to a report of three children lighting matches in the 1300 block of Hilltop Parkway.

• • • • • • • • • • • • • • • •

Aug. 9

5:35 a.m. Officers were called to a report of a convenience store employee who found a bag of marijuana in the 1800 block of Kamar Plaza. It later was discovered to be pipe tobacco.

2:30 p.m. Officers were called to a report of a person who was dumping sewage into a drain illegally from a motor home at Yampa and Seventh streets. It turned out to be clean water that was leaking from the motor home.

• • • • • • • • • • • • • • • •

Aug. 10

9:19 p.m. Officers were called to a report of a suspicious incident in the 1400 block of Pine Grove Road. An intoxicated man reported finding a hole in the ceiling above his bed. Officers said there was nothing suspicious about the hole.

• • • • • • • • • • • • • • • •

Aug. 15

2:57 p.m. Officers were called to a report of a disturbance in the 400 block of Lincoln Avenue. A business owner yelled at a cyclist for riding on the sidewalk, and officers helped mediate the argument.

10:54 p.m. Officers were called to a report of an unknown animal stuck in a Dumpster in the 2800 block of Riverside Plaza. It was a bear, and officers helped it get out.

• • • • • • • • • • • • • • • •

Aug. 16

8:45 a.m. Officers were called to a report of a woman who was threatened in the 1900 block of Cornice Road. The woman said a co-worker had put arsenic in her air vents in an attempt to poison her. Police think the report was unfounded.

Aug. 16

4:52 p.m. A person came to the police department and reported a fraud. The person said tickets had been sold to high school parents for a cheerleading clinic, and the clinic never was held.

. . . .

Aug. 17

2:20 a.m. Steamboat Springs Police Department officers contacted a suspicious man pushing a cart in the 600 block of Lincoln Avenue. The man claimed a bank stole his money.

. . . .

Aug. 18

8:45 a.m. Officers were called to a report of a hot air balloon that landed in someone's yard in the 1100 block of Anglers Drive. The homeowner called police to report the balloon was trespassing on his or her property. The pilot told police "they would never land there again."

. . . .

Aug. 19

2:33 p.m. Officers were called to a report of an assault at a local golf club. Police said a woman from Steamboat Springs allegedly punched a man from Denver during a fight that started after the woman confronted the man and said she was upset the man's golfing party was "not putting the flags back in the holes properly." The man who was punched didn't require medical attention, and no charges were pursued as a result of the incident.

Aug. 22

11:25 p.m. Officers were called to a report of a stolen car at Fifth Street and Lincoln Avenue. The woman's car had been taken by her boyfriend, and she did not want to press charges. The woman got upset, however, and threw her boyfriend's bag containing a $500 camera into the river. The boyfriend wanted to press charges, and the 35-year-old Longmont woman was arrested on suspicion of criminal mischief and theft.

. . . .

Aug. 27

1:09 p.m. Officers were called to help a person who had a fur coat stolen from a hotel last year in the 2300 block of Mount Werner Circle. The person wanted help in obtaining security camera footage. The footage no longer was available.

. . . .

Aug. 28

10:42 p.m. Officers were called to a report of a suspicious incident in Steamboat. A man reported a person was after him and trying to pull him out of his body. He was referred to mental health officials.

. . . .

Aug. 29

11:53 p.m. West Routt Fire Protection District firefighters were called to a report of a fire at Hayden Town Park. Three rolls of toilet paper had been set on fire, and the fire was put out by three juveniles in the area.

. . . .

Aug. 31

6:30 p.m. Officers were called to a report of the sound of gunshots and a person reloading a gun on Walton Pond Circle. The noise came from a bike tube that exploded while being inflated.

Aug. 31

8:24 p.m. Officers were called to a noise complaint in the 2400 block of Ski Trail Lane. It was a wedding party, and people were banging on bongo drums. They were told to not be so loud.

· · · · · · · · · · · · · · · ·

Sept. 2

2:05 p.m. Officers were called to a report of a man yelling at a child in the Walton Village Condos. When officers arrived, they discovered the man was yelling because his fish tank was making a mess, and a TV was on in the background.

· · · · · · · · · · · · · · · ·

Sept. 6

9:17 p.m. Officers were called to a report of a person in a car who was following around bears in the Cypress Court area.

· · · · · · · · · · · · · · · ·

Sept. 7

10:13 a.m. An officer came across a car in the middle of Pine Grove Road with no driver and its flashers on. The officer discovered that the car belonged to an employee of a nearby business who didn't know it was there because a coworker had moved it into the middle of the road as a prank. The prankster was warned.

· · · · · · · · · · · · · · · ·

Sept. 17

9:40 p.m. Officers were called to a report of a suspicious incident in the 2400 block of Lincoln Avenue. A person in a car was taking video of the jail. The person could not be found.

· · · · · · · · · · · · · · · ·

Sept. 18

8:14 a.m. Steamboat Spring Police Department officers and Steamboat Springs Fire Rescue firefighters were called to a report of a car on fire at Steamboat Springs High School. A squirrel had made a nest under the hood of the car, and it caught fire.

Sept. 28

1:43 p.m. Deputies were called to a report of harassment in the 200 block of South Sharp Avenue in Oak Creek. A man knocked on a person's door, asked weird questions and then asked for a glass of water. The man was given a glass of water and then said something threatening. The man was told to leave, and he ran away.

· · · · · · · · · · · · · · · ·

Oct. 2

12:54 p.m. Officers were called to a report of a woman who said her neighbor was not being nice to her in the 2400 block of Lincoln Avenue.

· · · · · · · · · · · · · · · ·

Oct. 5

5:23 p.m. Deputies were called to a report of a suspicious incident in the 30300 block of Triple Crown Lane. A man entered a house holding a briefcase and said he was there on horse-related business. The man hung out for a while and then drove away. He could not be found.

· · · · · · · · · · · · · · · ·

Oct. 8

11:59 a.m. Officers were called to a report of bears that got into the back of a car and were going through groceries in the 600 block of Meadowbrook Circle. They were gone when officers arrived.

· · · · · · · · · · · · · · · ·

Oct. 10

10:15 a.m. Officers were called to a report of a Mitt Romney campaign sign that had a phallic image drawn on it near Old Fish Creek Falls Road.

Oct. 12

6:26 p.m. Officers were called to a report of a porcupine stuck in the wheel well of a car in the 2000 block of Curve Plaza.

Oct. 15

11:11 a.m. Deputies were called to a report of a portable toilet knocked over on Buffalo Pass. The person who reported it wanted deputies to make sure no one was inside.

. . . .

Oct. 20

4:18 p.m. Officers were called to a report of a suspicious incident at Ninth Street and Lincoln Avenue. Someone called police to report a man playing a trumpet downtown was acting suspiciously. Officers contacted the man and determined he wasn't doing anything wrong.

. . . .

Oct. 21

9:29 p.m. Officers were called to a report of a woman who returned from being out of town and found a raccoon in her home in the 400 block of Blue Bell Court. The woman had tried pushing the raccoon out with a broom but was unsuccessful. The raccoon left before officers arrived.

. . . .

Oct. 24

3:01 p.m. Officers were called to a report of a suspicious person in the 700 block of Oak Street. A woman reported that a man walked into her salon and began taking off his clothes. The woman locked herself in the bathroom and called police. The man was located near Soda Creek Elementary School, where he was going to pick up his son. The man told police he walked into the salon to take his shirt off because he thought there was a spider in it, and he thought it was inappropriate to take his shirt off in public. The man was told not to return to the salon.

. . . .

Oct. 27

9:44 p.m. Officers were called to a report of a man in a cow costume harassing people in the 50 block of Seventh Street. Officers were not able to locate the man.

Nov. 6

1:57 p.m. Routt County Sheriff's Office deputies were called to a report of a suspicious person at a school in the 27200 block of Brandon Circle. A man was seen going to the school and trying to open two locked doors. The man then drove away. Deputies contacted the man, and he reported that he thought his election polling location was at the school.

. . . .

Nov. 12

4:30 p.m. Officers were called to a report of a suspicious incident in the 900 block of Weiss Drive. Two juveniles were seen walking with a 20-foot piece of pipe.

. . . .

Nov. 15

7:38 a.m. Steamboat Springs Police Department officers were called to a report of an unruly customer at a hotel in the 3100 block of Ingles Lane. A guest was upset about the amount of tax he was expected to pay. The guest left and was asked not to come back to the hotel.

. . . .

Nov. 18

4:45 a.m. Officers cited a Steamboat man for possessing alcohol as a minor in the 700 block of Yampa Street. Police said they witnessed the 20-year-old man drinking at a bar about an hour and a half before his 21st birthday.

. . . .

Nov. 22

10:04 p.m. Officers were called to a report of snowmaking guns being too loud in the 2900 block of Trails Edge. A man called officers and said he could not sleep and would break the snowmaking guns if they were not turned off. Officers talked to snowmaking personnel from Steamboat Ski Area, and they turned off the guns.

Nov. 25

9:47 a.m. Officers were called to a report of a naked elderly man stretching outside on a hotel room balcony in the 2200 block of Village Inn Court. Police were unable to locate the man.

. . . .

Dec. 1

2:13 p.m. Officers were called to a report of a suspicious man who was growling like a tiger at bar patrons in the 700 block of Lincoln Avenue. Police told the man he needed to leave the establishment.

. . . .

Dec. 13

11:24 p.m. Officers were called to a report of a disturbance at a movie theater in the 500 block of Marketplace Plaza. A drunken man was causing a scene because he wanted the midnight showing of "The Hobbit" to start early. The man was escorted out of the theater.

. . . .

Dec. 16

5:41 p.m. Officers were called to a report of a suspicious incident in the 800 block of Lincoln Avenue. A man found a blue plastic container on a bench. No other information was available.

. . . .

Dec. 17

1:03 p.m. Officers were called to a report of a man in the 800 block of Weiss Circle who was talking about weird things and conspiracy theories.

. . . .

Dec. 20

12:55 p.m. Officers were called to a report of fraud in the 1100 block of Hilltop Parkway. A sock company reported that socks that had not been released to the public were being sold on eBay. The company was investigating whether employees at a sock mill on the East Coast were stealing the socks.

Dec. 21

11:50 a.m. Officers were called to a report of a person who was selling a generator for a suspiciously low price in the 400 block of Lincoln Avenue.

. . . .

Dec. 22

1:33 p.m. Animal control officers were called to a report of a woman feeding popcorn to a hairless fox in the Ace at the Curve parking lot.

. . . .

Dec. 25

6:32 p.m. Steamboat firefighters were called to a report of a fire in the 300 block of Little Moon Trail. People using sparklers inside a townhome caught a Christmas tree on fire. A hose was used to put the fire out. The heat from the fire caused some windows to crack and melted a ceiling fan and TV.

. . . .

Dec. 28

7:33 p.m. Routt County Sheriff's Office deputies were called to the 29000 block of Routt County Road 64, where an argument about bringing alcohol onto a sleigh for a sleigh-ride dinner escalated between a family and staff members of a guest ranch. The family did not end up taking a sleigh to dinner and got a taxi back to Steamboat Springs.

. . . .

Dec. 31

10:20 p.m. Officers were called to a report of people in the 700 block of Marketplace Plaza who were upset because they could not get on a bus because it was full.

· · · · · · · · 2013 · · · · · · · ·

April 19

10:05 p.m. Police received a call from a woman who said her juvenile granddaughter was at the ski area and ran into a person who was selling bags of what she thought were portobello mushrooms dipped in chocolate for $30. Police said the granddaughter further informed her grandmother that giraffes were chasing her down the hill after she ate the mushrooms.

Featured in "Headlines" segment on "The Jay Leno Show!"

Jan. 2

12:53 a.m. Steamboat Springs Fire Rescue firefighters were called to a report of a possible structure fire in the 3100 block of Columbine Drive. A man had put a pan with oil on the stove and then had fallen asleep. Neighbors called for help when the fire alarm went off. There was a lot of smoke but no fire.

• • • • • • • • • • • • • • •

Jan. 9

1:20 a.m. Officers were called to do extra patrols at the ice castle because beer bottles and cans were found in the area. Officers found a person in the castle after it had closed, and the person gave police a fake name and birthdate and then ran from police. A 25-year-old was arrested for second-degree criminal trespassing, false reporting and obstructing a peace officer.

• • • • • • • • • • • • • • •

Jan. 20

3:35 p.m. Officers were called to a report of a group of seven people ages 19 to 21 trespassing in the 2000 block of Storm Meadows Drive. Police said the trespassers were trying to film a snowboarding video. Before they fled the scene in a vehicle, the group tried to throw snowballs at the person who called police.

• • • • • • • • • • • • • • •

Jan. 21

10:40 p.m. Officers were called to a report of two cowboys causing a disturbance at a bar in the 2200 block of Village Inn Court. Bar employees asked the cowboys to leave, but they did not want to leave. They eventually left, and officers contacted them. They were given a warning.

Feb. 5

7:19 p.m. Officers were called to a report of a suspicious incident in the 1300 block of Athens Plaza. A woman reported coming home and finding that someone had taken out her trash. Her door also was locked, which was strange because she does not lock her door.

• • • • • • • • • • • • • • •

Feb. 6

12:14 a.m. Steamboat Springs Police Department officers were called to help with a man who had been kicked out of a bar in the 700 block of Lincoln Avenue because he was drunk and causing a disturbance. The man was contacted and told not to return to the bar. About 30 minutes later, the man reportedly was fighting in front of the bar with another man who had been kicked out of the bar. A 23-year-old man and a 28-year-old man were arrested on suspicion of disorderly conduct.

6:18 p.m. Yampa Valley Regional Airport firefighters were called to a report of an aircraft emergency. A plane landed and then ran out of gas before being able to taxi off the runway. The runway was closed temporarily until the plane got off the runway. The pilot of the plane had intended to refuel at Steamboat Springs Airport but diverted to YVRA because of bad weather.

Feb. 10

12:54 a.m. Steamboat Springs Police Department officers were called to a report of a suspicious incident in the 700 block of Yampa Street. A visibly intoxicated woman was contacted coming out of a bar. She provided four different birthdates to officers. She was arrested on suspicion of minor in possession and false reporting.

. . . .

Feb. 11

4:12 p.m. Officers were called to a report of shoplifting from a grocery store in the 1800 block of Central Park Drive. A man reportedly went through the self-checkout lane and could not get his food stamp card to work. Police said the man then left without paying for the groceries. Police know who the man is because he left his wallet in the grocery store.

. . . .

Feb. 12

6:34 p.m. Officers were called to a report of underage females drinking at a bar in the 1100 block of Lincoln Avenue. Officers contacted the females, and they were in their early 30s.

Feb. 19

3:08 p.m. Oak Creek Fire Protection District firefighters were called to help rescue a dog that had climbed onto a roof and could not get down in the 400 block of North Grant Avenue. The fire chief lured the dog to the side of the roof using leftover birthday cake and then was able to grab onto the dog and get it off the roof.

. . . .

Feb. 22

6:19 p.m. Officers were called to a report of a suspicious man in the area of Central Park Plaza. The man reportedly had been hanging around for several hours and was staring. He was gone when officers arrived.

. . . .

Feb. 27

11:08 p.m. Officers were called to a report of a person who had friends who needed help because they were stuck in a set of handcuffs in the 2300 block of Storm Meadows Drive.

Jan. 31

9:36 p.m. Officers were called to help a person at a carwash business in the 100 block of Trafalgar Drive. A woman had her dog sprayed by a skunk, and she was using the self-service dog wash. The woman left the dog wash to get something out of her car, and when she returned, her dog was locked inside the dog wash. The owner of the car wash was contacted to unlock the door.

10:44 a.m. Officers were called to a report of a suspicious incident at a hotel in the 400 block of Lincoln Avenue. A man and woman reportedly had put $50 in the hotel office and took a key to a room. They thought it was a privilege afforded to local residents needing a place to stay. The couple then used the key to get into a room, and there was a man sleeping in the room. Police were able to identify the woman involved because she left her cellphone in the office. She was issued a summons for trespassing.

March 18

March 2

1:23 a.m. Steamboat Springs Police Department officers were called to a report of a man causing a disturbance at a convenience store on Anglers Drive. A clerk at the gas station called police after the man started yelling because the store didn't have any buns left for his hot dog.

March 3

1:53 a.m. Officers were called to a report of a suspicious incident in the 1100 block of South Lincoln Avenue. A group of men were seen waving a large American flag around on a Steamboat Springs Transit bus. Police later met up with the bus near Central Park Plaza, temporarily detained the men and determined the flag was stolen by someone else from a bar on Seventh Street.

· · · · · · · · · · · · · · · ·

March 5

4:04 p.m. Officers were called to a report of a suspicious incident in the 1500 block of Natches Way. A person thought it was suspicious that someone was flying a remote-controlled helicopter.

· · · · · · · · · · · · · · · ·

March 7

11:26 p.m. Officers were called to a report of a person who saw a driver roll his or her car onto its side on Hilltop Parkway. The driver got out, pushed the car back over and drove away. Officers later found the car, but the driver was not in it.

· · · · · · · · · · · · · · · ·

March 10

1:17 a.m. Steamboat Springs Police Department officers responded to a fight at Sixth Street and Lincoln Avenue. The two men, who described themselves as friends, said the fight began when one man spilled a hot dog and mustard on the other man. They were cited for municipal disorderly conduct.

· · · · · · · · · · · · · · · ·

March 11

5:39 a.m. Officers were called to a report of a car repeatedly driving around Moraine Circle. The driver was contacted, and she said she was driving around because she could not sleep.

March 15

2:40 p.m. Officers received an anonymous tip from a person who wanted to report that last year a person in Steamboat raised $7,000 by fraudulently telling people he or she had cancer.

. . . .

March 16

12:17 p.m. Officers were called to a report of a woman who said her pair of earrings worth $30,000 was stolen from her home in the 1700 block of Medicine Springs Drive. Police were able to locate the lost earrings in the bathroom in her residence.

. . . .

March 19

7:23 p.m. Officers followed up on a report of a man living in Steamboat who looked like Eric Toth, a man on the FBI's 10 Most Wanted list. Officers contacted a man in the 1200 block of Walton Creek Road, and it was not Toth.

. . . .

March 26

8:33 p.m. Deputies were called to a report of a suspicious incident on Spring Creek Trail. A mother called to say her 16-year-old daughter reported seeing what looked like the remains of a human leg bone on the side of the trail. The bone belonged to an elk.

. . . .

March 29

7:42 p.m. Officers were called to a report of a drunken person who was carrying groceries at Whistler Road and Meadow Lane. When officers arrived, the man dropped the groceries and ran into his house.

. . . .

April 5

1:42 a.m. Officers were called to a report of loud Spanish polka music in the first block of Anglers Drive.

April 6

11:19 a.m. Animal control officers in Steamboat were called to a complaint about three dogs sitting on the roof of a two-story home in the 200 block of Pine Street.

12:07 p.m. Animal control officers were called to a complaint about a husky dog on the roof of a building in the 1900 block of Alpine Plaza.

3:30 p.m. Officers were called to a report of a mobility scooter stolen from Walmart. Police found the scooter being driven by two 13-year-old girls at Seventh Street and Lincoln Avenue. The girls were taken into custody on suspicion of felony theft and released to responsible adults. The scooter was valued at more than $2,000.

. . . .

April 16

10:56 a.m. Officers were called to a report of a person who received a fraudulent phone call from someone who said he or she had won the lottery. After the person told the caller he or she thought the call was a scam, the person was cussed out.

April 19

9:07 a.m. Steamboat Springs Fire Rescue firefighters, mental health services and Routt County Sheriff's Office deputies were called to the 27000 block of Brandon Circle for a report of a woman who had crossed U.S. Highway 40 and taken off her clothes near a school because she wanted to swim in a pond. She was transported to Yampa Valley Medical Center.

1:09 p.m. Police were called to a report of a hot tub cover that had been vandalized while the home's owner was out of town. A sergeant advised that the suspect possibly was a bear.

. . . .

April 27

11:22 a.m. Officers were called to a report of a suspicious incident at Whistler Road and Covey Circle. A passerby called police after they found a small, dead alligator in a flower garden. Police weren't able to determine how the alligator got there but suspected it was someone's deceased pet. Colorado Parks and Wildlife officers were called to dispose of the approximately 18-inch long reptile because it was emitting a foul odor.

. . . .

May 6

6:55 p.m. Officers were called to a report of a woman who came home and found a drunken man on her car in the 2900 block of Columbine Drive. He walked away and seemed disoriented. He was carrying a trash can, and his pants were falling off. Officers could not find him.

. . . .

May 10

2:51 p.m. Officers were called to a report of a rollover accident in the 1800 block of Burgess Creek Road. The driver was trying to roll his or her car down a hill and pop the clutch to get the car started. The steering wheel locked up, so the driver was not able to control the car.

May 13

8:09 p.m. Officers were called to a report of a person in the 400 block of Willow Court who said his or her credit card had been used in a prison to buy a phone card.

. . . .

May 14

8:27 a.m. Steamboat Springs Police Department officers were called to a report of a bear that got into a Subaru after opening the unlocked car door in the 1800 block of Hunters Court. The bear defecated in the Subaru and chewed through a container of motor oil. According to police, some bears know how to open car doors.

. . . .

May 20

9:32 p.m. Officers were called to a report of a dispute between neighbors in the 400 block of Eighth Street. A man was reportedly irritated about a nightlight at his neighbor's house, and he had repeatedly gone over and unscrewed the light. The nightlight was used to keep bears and skunks away. Officers mediated the situation.

. . . .

May 29

2:33 a.m. Officers were called to a report of a bear that had locked itself inside a Subaru hatchback in the 2900 block of Ridge Road. The owner discovered the bear because the bear kept hitting the car's horn. Officers opened the car doors and let the bear out. The bear caused extensive damage to the car by chewing on the interior and clawing the roof.

11:04 a.m. Officers were called to a report of property found at a hotel in the 1100 block of Lincoln Avenue. A woman who stayed at the hotel in February had left her belongings, including her ex-husband's cremated remains. Police were going to mail the ex-husband's remains to his brother.

May 31

12:26 a.m. Steamboat Springs Police Department officers were called to a report of a disturbance in the 700 block of Lincoln Avenue. A drunken man was crying at the bar. The man's dad came to pick him up.

. . . .

June 1

11:35 a.m. Officers were called to a report of a bear that was chasing ducks in a pond in the 900 block of Mauna Kea Lane. The bear was gone when officers arrived.

. . . .

June 4

9:07 p.m. Officers were called to help a person who was concerned about an animal stuck in the exhaust fan above the oven in the 1300 block of Indian Trails. The tenant was told to call his or her landlord.

. . . .

June 6

7:56 a.m. Officers were called to a report of a bear that opened the doors of an unlocked Toyota 4Runner in the 2400 block of Ski Trail Lane. The bear got inside and damaged the center console and dash. Wildlife officers trapped a bear near the residence during the night.

. . . .

June 9

11:44 p.m. Officers were called to a report of a bear in the 2300 block of Mount Werner Circle. A bear was in the underground parking garage of The Steamboat Grand. When officers attempted to herd it out, the bear hid behind cars and did not want to leave the area.

. . . .

June 11

10:05 p.m. Officers were called to a report of a woman who was concerned about what she described as a group of gangsters in a moving van at Stock Bridge Transit Center. The people were contacted, and everything was fine.

May 20 — 11:44 p.m. Officers were called to a report of a bear trapped in a Dumpster in the 2200 block of Village Inn Court. Police sounded their siren and threw rocks at the bear. The bear jumped out of the Dumpster and ran away.

June 12

9:37 a.m. Officers were called to a report of a restaurant in the 400 block of Anglers Drive that put alcohol in a child's daiquiri drink that was supposed to be nonalcoholic. The mother reported the incident after her boy said his drink tasted funny. The incident was forwarded to the local liquor licensing authority.

. . . .

June 14

10:46 a.m. Officers were called to a report of a bear that went into a house and ate dog food in the 500 block of Pine Street.

. . . .

June 19

10:09 p.m. Officers were called to respond to Yampa Valley Medical Center for a woman that was bitten by a dog. The woman was the dog's owner. She said her 13-year-old deaf dachshund bit her on the lip because the dog was upset about a new puppy in the house.

June 20

11:23 p.m. Officers were called to a report of a suspicious person in the 2500 block of Ski Trail Lane. It was a police officer investigating an alarm.

• • • • • • • • • • • • • • •

June 27

11:19 p.m. Officers were called to a report of a noise complaint in the 600 block of Anglers Drive. A woman called to complain that her upstairs neighbor was stomping around and playing loud music. She said she thought he might be mad at her because she didn't give him a ride home after seeing him at the liquor store.

• • • • • • • • • • • • • • •

June 28

7:37 p.m. Officers responded to reports of a drunk pedestrian in the 800 block of Howelsen Parkway. Two females were issued minor in possession tickets after one ran out in the middle of a Little League game, stole a glove and threw it.

• • • • • • • • • • • • • • •

July 3

4:01 p.m. Officers were called to a report of a person selling sage sticks at Sixth Street and Lincoln Avenue. The person was gone when officers arrived.

July 4

2:35 a.m. Steamboat Springs Police Department officers were called to a report of fireworks at Little Moon Trail and Tamarack Drive. There were 14 other complaints about fireworks.

• • • • • • • • • • • • • • •

July 5

9:13 a.m. Officers were called to a report of a unicycle that had been stolen the previous night from a bar in the 700 block of Yampa Street.

2:56 p.m. Officers were called to a noise complaint at a house along a golf course in the 1200 block of Steamboat Boulevard. People in the house were being loud and taunting golfers. They were asked to be quiet.

• • • • • • • • • • • • • • •

July 12

7:56 a.m. Officers were called to a report of a hot air balloon chaser who was speeding near Chinook Lane. The chaser got in an argument with a resident and was given a summons for disorderly conduct.

July 7

11:36 a.m. A transient man told police two bear cubs stole his phone and his wallet from his makeshift campsite in the woods near the 1400 block of Pine Grove Road. Police said food at the man's campsite was likely attracting bears to the area but couldn't confirm whether any bears had taken the items or if they were lost in the woods. Police told the man it wasn't legal to camp in the area.

July 12

9:07 p.m. Officers were called to a report of a resident in the Fish Creek Falls Road area who wanted to complain about loud music coming from Howelsen Hill, where a free summer concert was being held.

. . . .

July 13

7:55 p.m. Officers were called to a suspicious incident in the 2300 block of Mount Werner Circle. A man was on top of the gondola while it was moving.

. . . .

July 16

5:08 p.m. Officers and Steamboat firefighters were called to help a 21-year-old woman who said she had been bitten by a big black spider. The woman flicked the spider off and did not know what kind it was. Firefighters did not take her to the hospital.

. . . .

July 18

11:14 p.m. Officers were called to a report of people having sex in a bathroom at a bar in the 600 block of Lincoln Avenue. Officers told the married couple not to return to the bar. They also were given summonses to appear in court for indecent exposure.

. . . .

July 22

2:39 p.m. Steamboat Springs Fire Rescue firefighters were called to a report of a wildfire at Fish Creek Falls Reservoir. An area about 4 inches in diameter was smoldering, according to the report. A U.S. Forest Service crew was going to investigate the fire.

. . . .

July 23

8:58 a.m. Officers were called to a report of a car that had been parked for two years in the 1800 block of Ski Time Square Drive. It was gone when officers arrived.

July 23

2:18 p.m. Officers were called to a report of a man hanging out of a car window and filming himself at Ninth Street and Lincoln Avenue. The man was contacted, and he was wearing a camouflage bandana and had a towel wrapped around his head. The man claimed to be an Islamic jihadist, but police determined this was unfounded.

. . . .

July 30

11:27 p.m. Officers were called to a report of a person who called police to say "people were being jerks" in the 2800 block of Village Drive. The person then hung up the phone.

. . . .

July 31

8:14 p.m. Officers were called to a report of a transient man who had repeatedly been taking coffee without paying for it at a gas station in the 500 block of Marketplace Plaza. The clerk confronted the man, who showed his middle finger and walked out.

. . . .

Aug. 1

8:45 p.m. Officers were called to a report of a theft in the 1800 block of Ski Time Square Drive. A "nice-looking" family consisting of a couple and their two kids left a restaurant without paying their $125 bill. Police could not find them.

10:47 p.m. Officers were called to a report of gunshots in the 2000 block of Walton Creek Road. A person reported hearing four shots and a ricochet and saw a flash. Eight people were seen running down the street and laughing, and one person was heard saying "well that hurt like hell." Another person saw three males with fireworks in the area.

Aug. 8

8:19 a.m. Officers were called to assist a person at Walton Village Condos. A woman who refused to give her name called to complain about a hot air balloon that landed in Sparta Plaza parking lot. She was concerned about the legality of where the balloon could land and said the flames were near buildings. Officers issued a verbal warning to the balloonist.

. . . .

Aug. 12

1:59 p.m. Officers were called to a report of a motel owner in the 1100 block of Lincoln Avenue who wanted to complain about a dog owner letting his or her dog go to the bathroom on motel property. The motel owner wanted to complain even though the dog owner cleaned up after the dog. Police did not do anything about it.

. . . .

Aug. 15

7:58 p.m. Officers were called to a report of a suspicious incident at Ski Trail Lane and Après Ski Way. Someone in a passing Ford Explorer shot a blowgun dart at a man riding home on his bicycle, and the dart stuck in the man's rear end. Officers were unable to locate the two men in the Explorer, who were described as being 20 to 30 years old.

. . . .

Aug. 25

8:14 p.m. Officers were called to a report of a suspicious shirtless man who was walking into traffic at Walton Creek and Whistler roads. The man, who also was not wearing any shoes, was gone when officers arrived.

. . . .

Aug. 26

5:42 p.m. Deputies were called to a report of a person with a gun at a golf course in the 26800 block of U.S. Highway 40. It was a golf course employee hunting a gopher.

Aug. 28

12:16 p.m. Officers were called to a report of a person who saw a woman driving a white Ford Explorer while drinking wine out of a bottle at Fourth Street and Lincoln Avenue. Officers could not find the woman.

. . . .

Aug. 29

4:44 a.m. Steamboat Springs Police Department officers were called to a report of males who were loud and had been jumping on a trampoline for the past seven hours in the 400 block of Eighth Street.

. . . .

Aug. 30

10:44 a.m. Officers were called to a report of a person who wanted to complain about a neighbor who had roosters and chickens on his or her patio.

. . . .

Sept. 3

1:38 p.m. Officers were called to a report of a woman who stole a box of pain medication from a grocery store in the 1800 block of Central Park Drive. The woman also reportedly tried to steal chicken, but it would not fit in her bag, so she put it back.

5:57 p.m. Routt County Sheriff's Office deputies were called to a report of neighbors who were having an argument about fence lines and cattle in the 6100 block of Routt County Road 74A near Hayden.

. . . .

Sept. 5

5:00 p.m. Officers were called to a report of a bike that had been locked up for a week in the 1100 block of South Lincoln Avenue. The bike belonged to a man who had been arrested and was in jail.

2:13 p.m. Deputies were called to a report of a possibly drunken woman who defecated in a neighbor's yard in the 200 block of Wild Hogg Drive in Oak Creek. A 44-year-old woman was arrested for failing to appear in court.

June 21

Sept. 8

4:13 p.m. Officers were called to a report of a suspicious car in the 2300 block of Lincoln Avenue. A person called to report a truck was parked with a tarp over the bed, and a man was underneath the tarp using a computer. Officers contacted the man, and he was trying to use the Wi-Fi from a nearby business.

Sept. 9

10:11 a.m. Officers were called to a report at a bar in the 600 block of Lincoln Avenue. A 27-year-old man broke into the bar after it closed, drank beer and liquor and then passed out in the basement office. He was arrested.

Sept. 20

2:54 p.m. Officers were called to a report of a stolen car at a hotel in the 2300 block of Mount Werner Circle. Police said a man took a rental car from the valet, drove it around and returned it. The man told police he "wanted to see what happened." Police said they think the man was under the influence of drugs and possibly was suffering from mental health issues. A 62-year-old man was arrested on suspicion of aggravated motor vehicle theft.

Sept. 23

10:28 p.m. Officers were called to a report of harassment in the 500 block of Wyatt Drive. A man reportedly had asked his neighbor to turn off a porch light so he could see the stars. When the neighbor did not turn off the porch light, the man became belligerent. Officers contacted the man and told him to behave.

Sept. 27

10:54 p.m. Steamboat Springs Fire Rescue firefighters were called to help a person bleeding at a bar in the 700 block of Yampa Street. A drunken man passed out while going to the bathroom and hit his head on the urinal. He was taken to Yampa Valley Medical Center with a facial laceration.

Sept. 28

9:55 p.m. Officers were called to a report of two males wearing black-and-white spandex and jumping on a car in a parking lot in the 1800 block of Central Park Drive. They could not be found.

Oct. 9

9:47 a.m. Officers were called to a report of vandalism at a Fetcher Park bathroom. The door handle and lock had been taken off a door. Reportedly, a woman removed the handle and lock because she got locked in the bathroom the previous night. The lock is automatic and locks starting at 8 p.m. The woman did not see a button that bypasses the timer and allows people to get out if they are locked in.

8:10 p.m. Officers were called to check on a woman in the 700 block of Tamarack Drive. A person was concerned that a woman was very drunk with her two children. Police discovered the woman sounded drunk because she had pneumonia.

Oct. 11

9:06 p.m. Officers were called to a report of theft at Colorado Mountain College. A male employee reported $9,000 in cash had been taken from a backpack he left inside his office. The man said only one other person knew the money was there. The man did not want to say why he had the large amount of cash.

• • • • • • • • • • • • • • • •

Oct. 14

9:55 a.m. Steamboat Springs Police Department officers were called to a report of trespassing at a radio station in the 2900 block of Village Drive. For the past several months, a local woman had been hanging out in the lobby, using the restrooms and storing food in the business's refrigerator. The employees did not want her hanging around anymore.

Sept. 6

2:47 p.m. Officers were called to a report of a suspicious incident in the 1800 block of Central Park Drive. A man and a woman with dreadlocks and two dogs were skinning a raccoon in the parking lot. Officers could not find them. Coincidentally, a man had called earlier in the day to ask if he could skin a deer in the same parking lot. He was told that while not illegal, it probably was not a good idea.

Oct. 24

11:05 p.m. Officers were called to a report of a drunken person behind a bar in the first block of Seventh Street. The 30-year-old man was upset over the Red Sox losing Game 2 of the World Series. He was taken to Yampa Valley Medical Center.

• • • • • • • • • • • • • • • •

Oct. 26

4:11 p.m. Officers were called to a suspicious incident on the 800 block of Mill Run Court. The caller reported seeing someone climb a power pole. The climber then climbed back down.

• • • • • • • • • • • • • • • •

Oct. 30

7:44 a.m. Steamboat Springs Police Department officers were called to a report of graffiti in the 800 block of Oak Street. Police followed other cases of graffiti to a home on Merritt Street, and they found a pumpkin decorated with similar graffiti. Police contacted a 22-year-old man who lived there, and he admitted to spraying the graffiti. The man was arrested on suspicion of felony criminal mischief.

• • • • • • • • • • • • • • • •

Nov. 4

9:53 a.m. Officers were called to a report of a business owner who said $4,000 in cash had been taken out of his car somewhere in Steamboat a couple of months ago. The business owner was just getting around to reporting the missing money.

• • • • • • • • • • • • • • • •

Nov. 8

11:02 p.m. Steamboat Springs Police Department officers responded to a report of criminal mischief in the 1300 block of Lincoln Avenue, where there were reports of spray painting. Officers contacted two women dressed in all black, and both women's hands were wet with paint. Both were arrested.

Nov. 10

12:18 p.m. Officers were called to a report of a bear in the 1300 block of Bob Adams Drive. A man was walking on Colorado Mountain College's campus when he saw a bear. He dropped his sweater near the bear when leaving the area and called police to retrieve the sweater. The sweater was returned to him.

1:35 p.m. Deputies were called to a report of a suspicious incident in the 24000 block of Rawhide Trail. A man called to report that a plane flying overhead was causing his horses to run. The plane left the area.

. . . .

Nov. 15

2:23 a.m. Officers responded to a suspicious incident in the 1100 block of Lincoln Avenue. Two men were beating a car with baseball bats. Officers contacted them, and one of the men proved it was his car. The man said they were going to scrap the car the next day. Officers asked them to stop.

10:50 a.m. Officers responded to a report of shoplifting in the 1800 block of Central Park Drive. A man stole $24.29 worth of merchandise. He told officers he had a job interview and needed a toothbrush. He was given a citation.

. . . .

Nov. 25

12:24 p.m. Officers were called to a report of shoplifting at a grocery store in the 1800 block of Central Park Drive. Someone had put food items, including steaks and a rack of lamb, in his or her backpack. A summons was issued to appear in court.

2:37 p.m. Officers were called to a report of theft in the 1600 block of Natches Way. A resident reported someone stole $4,000 worth of silverware and dinnerware in late September or October.

Nov. 29

10:20 p.m. Officers were called to a report of a man who was refusing to pay his bar tab for $26.75 in the 800 block of Lincoln Avenue. He was placed in custody but let go after the man's mother came and paid the tab.

. . . .

Dec. 4

12:07 a.m. Steamboat Springs Police Department officers were called to a report of a disturbance at a bar in the 700 block of Yampa Street. A drunken man became upset after being cut off by the bartender. While being escorted out of the bar, he poured a beer on a customer. Once outside the bar, the bartender said the man broke a beer bottle and threw snowballs at the bar window. Police found the man walking down Lincoln Avenue carrying a yellow sled, and he reportedly had a collapsible baton in his pocket. Police said he made threatening remarks to an officer while being taken to jail. The 35-year-old man was arrested on suspicion of felony attempting to influence a public servant, possession of a dangerous weapon, resisting an officer and disorderly conduct.

. . . .

Dec. 8

12:41 a.m. Officers spotted a man riding on the back of a Colorado Department of Transportation snowplow at Walton Creek Road and U.S. Highway 40. After he was spotted, the man jumped off the vehicle and tried to run from the police. Police caught up with the man nearby and determined he was intoxicated. The man said he rode on the plow from downtown to Walton Pond. The man was issued a ticket for illegally riding on the back of a vehicle.

trespassing in one of the bars he had been kicked out of the day before.

Dec. 17

3:21 p.m. Officers were called to a report of a suspicious person at the Steamboat Springs Chamber Resort Association. A homeless man had been hanging out in the area, and Chamber staff members said he was not the sort of ambassador they wanted for Steamboat. The man left the area when officers arrived.

• • • • • • • • • • • • • • •

Dec. 18

12:08 a.m. Steamboat Springs Police Department officers were called to a report of a suspicious man wearing chef pants who was claiming to be a mixed martial arts fighter and offering to give marijuana to people in the 600 block of Lincoln Avenue. The transient man had been kicked out of three downtown bars the night before. He later was arrested at about 11:53 p.m. for

Dec. 24

2:13 p.m. Officers were called to a report of a missing person at a Mexican restaurant on Snapdragon Way. A man said he went to the bathroom, and his wife was gone when he returned. The wife had a 2:30 p.m. hair appointment, and she was located at a salon in Marketplace Plaza.

• • • • • • • • • • • • • • •

Dec. 27

9:13 a.m. Officers were called to a report of a person who wanted to complain about a truck idling in an alley in the 600 block of Lincoln Avenue. The person thought it was bad for the environment. The truck was gone when officers arrived.

2:29 p.m. Officers were called to a report of a civil situation at a hotel in the 3100 block of Ingles Lane. Two women were staying in a room, and one wanted the other to pay for damages related to a stain on the bed.

Nov. 3

9:25 p.m. Officers were called to a report of a drunken man who had removed all of his clothes except for his underwear at a bus stop at Snow Bowl Plaza. The 30-year-old man took off his shirt while riding the bus. The bus then became stuck at the Snow Bowl Plaza stop, and while the driver waited for assistance, the drunken man took off his pants, shoes and socks outside. The bus driver called police, and officers arrested the man for disorderly conduct. Police said they had contacted the same man twice earlier in the day for soliciting money from customers at a store in Central Park Plaza.

2014

June 5

8:18 a.m. Steamboat Springs Police Department officers were called to a report of a suspicious incident. An elementary school student reported seeing a "creepy guy" at the carnival.

Jan. 1

1:56 a.m. Officers were called to a report of a man in a tuxedo fighting in the 700 block of Yampa Street.

• • • • • • • • • • • • • • • •

Jan. 2

8:51 p.m. Officers were called to a report of a suspicious person at a church in the 500 block of Oak Street. A person reported finding a man who was drunk or high in a stairwell. The man reportedly said he was "going to feed the magpies, and Jesus was going to save the world." Police contacted the man, and the church had given him permission to be there.

• • • • • • • • • • • • • • • •

Jan. 5

11:28 a.m. Officers were called to a report of a Mercedes that had been keyed in the 1100 block of Bangtail Way. The person who keyed the vehicle also left two notes, one with an expletive and another that read, "Just because you drive a Mercedes doesn't entitle you to take up two spots." Police were unable to locate the person responsible for the vandalism.

1:57 p.m. Officers were called to a report of a suspicious man at Walton Creek and Whistler roads who was hitchhiking and pushing ice into the road. The man told police he was trying to build a snowman. Police told him he couldn't build it in the road and needed to remove the block of ice.

9:30 p.m. Officers were called to a report of a drunken person who was passed out and snoring in a bathroom stall at a tavern in the 700 block of Yampa Street.

2:51 a.m. Officers were called to a report of a suspicious car that was running in the 1500 block of Shadow Run Court. A man was sleeping in the car. He said he fell asleep while talking to his girlfriend on the phone.

Jan 8

12:53 a.m. Steamboat Springs Police Department officers were called to a report of a bobcat pelt wall decoration stolen from a bar in the first block of Seventh Street.

• • • • • • • • • • • • • • • •

Jan. 17

2:35 p.m. Officers were called to a report of a theft in the 300 block of Lincoln Avenue. A flock of plastic pink flamingos had been placed there overnight as part of a nonprofit fundraiser, and the flamingos were stolen. Police did not have any suspects.

• • • • • • • • • • • • • • • •

Feb. 7

10:55 a.m. Officers were called to a report of two people who had gotten into an argument about dog poop in the 2600 block of Copper Ridge Circle.

• • • • • • • • • • • • • • • •

Feb. 27

7:10 p.m. Officers were called to a report of a suspicious incident in the 800 block of Yampa Street. A parent reported that his or her child was playing a game of Minecraft online when the person the child was playing with said he or she was "coming to get them." The parent wanted the incident documented by police.

March 6

9:52 p.m. Officers were called to a report of a snowcat at Howelsen Hill that had been moved from where it had been parked. The keys had been left in it, and someone took it joyriding. It was located on the other side of the hill, and it was not damaged.

March 12

1:04 p.m. Officers were called to a report of a disturbance between roommates in the 800 block of South Lincoln Avenue. The disturbance started when the roommates were having "childish stereo volume wars."

• • • • • • • • • • • • • • • •

March 13

6:20 p.m. Officers were called to a report of people in Whistler Park who were hitting golf balls toward people on the Yampa River Core Trail. The person who reported it said one of the people hitting balls wanted to start a fight when they were asked to stop.

12:34 a.m. Officers were called to a report of a disturbance at a hotel in the 2300 block of Mount Werner Circle. A man reportedly was running around in a bikini and exposing himself. A 33-year-old man was arrested on suspicion of two counts of indecent exposure.

Jan. 6

March 20

1:41 a.m. Steamboat Springs Police Department officers were called to a report of a man urinating at a bus stop at Lincoln Avenue and Fifth Street. Officers found evidence of urination, but the man was gone.

• • • • • • • • • • • • • • •

March 21

12:26 p.m. Officers were called to a report of a suspicious incident in the 2600 block of Windward Way. A homeowner was away and called home to get voicemails. Someone answered the phone. No one was there when officers arrived, and it did not look like anything was disturbed.

Jan. 17

10:58 p.m. Officers were called to help a man looking for his daughter. While looking for the daughter, they contacted a man in a car at 10th Street and Lincoln Avenue. Police thought he was under the influence of something. The 18-year-old was arrested on suspicion of felony possession of a controlled substance. On the way to the jail, police said the man was doing somersaults in the back seat of the police car and scratching himself because he thought spiders were crawling on him.

March 22

8:54 a.m. Officers were called to a suspicious incident in the 700 block of Critter Court. Someone broke into an animal shelter when it was closed and took back his dog, which had been taken by animal control earlier.

• • • • • • • • • • • • • • •

March 24

3:07 p.m. Officers were called to a report of a woman who was driving all across the road while putting on makeup at Yampa and 10th streets. The woman eventually parked. Officers contacted her and gave her a warning.

• • • • • • • • • • • • • • •

March 25

9:30 a.m. Officers were called to a report of a two-car crash near Hilltop Parkway and Falling Water Lane. Two people went to Yampa Valley Medical Center with minor injuries. A driver was given a ticket for careless driving and not wearing a seat belt. The driver had leaned over to pick up a CD and swerved into the oncoming lane.

• • • • • • • • • • • • • • •

April 1

2:25 p.m. Officers were called to a report of a teenage male who had covered his license plate with foil in the 3100 block of Willowbrook Court. The teen said he covered his license plate because he thought a man was looking at him funny. The teen was told it was illegal to cover his license plate.

4:57 p.m. Officers were called to a report of a moose at Steamboat Springs High School.

• • • • • • • • • • • • • • •

April 7

4:56 p.m. Officers were called to a report of a car going about 40 mph on Sparta Plaza in a condo complex. The person who reported it thought teenagers were trying to get air off speed bumps.

April 7

11:04 p.m. Officers were called to help a person at a convenience store in the 2000 block of Curve Plaza. A clerk was having problems with a customer. Police told the customer not to return. He returned, and the clerk reportedly was scared because the customer was shadow boxing. The 31-year-old man was arrested on suspicion of third-degree criminal trespassing and obstructing a peace officer.

. . . .

April 9

6:10 p.m. Officers were called to a report of a man who tried to leave a grocery store in the 1800 block of Central Park Drive without paying for Q-tips. When security told the man he was not in trouble, he ran away and could not be located.

. . . .

April 13

6:28 p.m. Officers were called to a report of theft at a gas station in the 500 block of Marketplace Plaza. Some people who had hitched a ride to Steamboat from Vail left the stranger's car to use the bathroom. The car then drove away with the people's personal belongings inside. The victims, who were attending a concert, told police they had $20,000 worth of jewelry and other personal belongings in the car that drove away. Police said they were working on some leads to find the suspects.

. . . .

April 22

9:56 a.m. Steamboat Springs Police Department officers were called to a report of harassment in the 600 block of Tamarack Drive. A woman complained that her neighbor wouldn't let their children play together. The woman who reported this to police thought the situation was harassment.

April 30

1:19 a.m. Officers were called to a report by a woman who said someone was in her yard doing magic or witchcraft in the 400 block of Pitkin Street.

7:22 p.m. Officers were called to a report of a wallet found in the 600 block of Harms Court. The wallet was reported missing in 2004. It still contained cards and money, but the money was moldy, and it looked like an animal had chewed on the wallet. Officers were trying to locate the owner.

. . . .

May 1

4:13 p.m. Officers were called to help a person who said someone directing traffic at Walton Creek Road and South Lincoln Avenue posted a picture of his or her car on Facebook and said he or she was a bad driver.

. . . .

May 12

4:29 p.m. Officers were called to a report of a disturbance at a dog washing facility in the 100 block of Trafalgar Drive. A woman was inside the dog wash trying to get her credit card to work. A man then opened the door, and her dog got out. Words were then exchanged.

. . . .

May 16

12:06 a.m. Steamboat Springs Police Department officers were called to a report of a woman who said a bear was in her garbage, and when she tried to scare it off, it tried to charge her in the 300 block of Cherry Lane. The bear left the area.

. . . .

May 19

9:14 p.m. Officers were called to check on a man sleeping on lawn furniture at a store in the 1800 block of Central Park Drive. The man was contacted.

7:26 a.m. Steamboat Springs Police Department officers were called to a report of an open door at a dentist office in the 1400 block of Pine Grove Road. Someone had used a crowbar to open the back door, and a tank of nitrous oxide was stolen. **May 9**

June 4

4:59 p.m. Officers were called to a report of a suspicious incident at a business in the 1800 block of Central Park Drive. A man reportedly was doing sexual things in the bathroom, and another man tried to give the man $5 to make him go away. The man eventually left. Video surveillance footage was being reviewed.

. . . .

June 5

8:24 p.m. Officers were called to a report of a woman who was concerned about a man seen coming out of a business in the 1800 block of Central Park Drive with an armload of ammunition.

. . . .

June 6

8:45 p.m. Officers contacted a couple who could not figure out how to use the gas pumps at a station in the first block of Anglers Drive. They were shown how to use the pumps.

. . . .

June 7

11:06 a.m. The manager of the Alpine slide at Howelsen Hill called to report a customer was upset about his experience on the slide. Officers didn't take a report.

. . . .

June 12

12:35 p.m. Officers were called to a report of shoplifting at a grocery store in the 1800 block of Central Park Drive. A man reportedly tried to steal $40 worth of light bulbs by putting them under his hat. He was given a citation.

May 25

12:46 p.m. Officers were called to a report of trespassing in the 3000 block of Après Ski Way. A family returned home from vacation to find a person sleeping in their house.

. . . .

May 27

11:33 p.m. Officers contacted a suspicious car at Clearwater Trail. Two people were being romantic, and they were told to relocate.

. . . .

June 1

6:16 p.m. Officers were called to a report of a suspicious incident in the 800 block of Howelsen Parkway. A softball team was practicing and hitting several home runs over the fence. The balls were landing in the volleyball and tennis court areas, disturbing other players.

. . . .

June 2

2:42 p.m. Officers were called to a report of three Lamborghinis being driven recklessly at Shield Drive and Curve Plaza. They could not be located.

June 17

10:18 p.m. Officers were called to a report of a suspicious car in the 1500 block of Secluded Court. The car was unoccupied, but officers saw three males who were trying to hide in some shrubs. A bag of marijuana was on the ground, and two citations were issued for underage possession of marijuana.

• • • • • • • • • • • • • • •

June 18

8:18 p.m. Officers were called to a report of several kids chasing a bear in the 1400 block of Pine Grove Road. An adult told them to stop, but the kids did not listen. The bear eventually ran away.

• • • • • • • • • • • • • • •

June 25

1:16 p.m. Officers were called to a report of a suspicious person at Anglers Drive and South Lincoln Avenue. A man was holding a sign that was asking people to hit him with quarters. Traffic was being disrupted because of the activity.

• • • • • • • • • • • • • • •

July 4

7:02 p.m. Officers were called to a report of a homeless person going through a Dumpster and finding things to eat in the 600 block of Lincoln Avenue.

• • • • • • • • • • • • • • •

July 6

9:00 p.m. A person called police claiming there were too many people in a theater in the 800 block of Lincoln Avenue and that the situation was against the fire code.

• • • • • • • • • • • • • • •

July 7

10:37 p.m. Officers were called to a report of a person who wanted to complain about people yelling and cheering too loudly at a baseball game at Howelsen Hill. Nothing was done about the complaint.

July 13

8:35 a.m. Officers were called to a report of a moose and her calf trying to cross U.S. Highway 40 in the 300 block of Mount Werner Road.

4:07 p.m. Officers were called to a report of a man smoking marijuana near a red motorcycle at Howelsen Hill. The man tried to walk away from police when they arrived. The man had two outstanding warrants. The motorcycle was reported stolen from California. Officers arrested the 28-year-old man on suspicion of felony theft and on the outstanding warrants. He also was ticketed for consuming marijuana in public.

• • • • • • • • • • • • • • •

July 19

12:36 p.m. Officers were called to a disturbance at the Yampa River Botanic Park. It was reported a soccer team was walking through the flowers at the garden. When confronted by a patron, the situation escalated into a disturbance, and everyone was separated when officers arrived. A report was taken.

4:24 p.m. Officers were called to a report of a disturbance at the Emerald Fields. A parent was ejected by officials from a soccer game. The parent tried to sneak back into the game and was confronted by the officials. A spectator called officers to respond to the disturbance.

• • • • • • • • • • • • • • •

July 22

9:36 p.m. Officers were called to a report of a bear that ripped open a storm door in the 1700 block of Brome Drive. The resident sprayed the bear with pepper spray, and the bear left.

July 28

10:57 p.m. Officers were called to a report of a homeowner who discovered a bear eating pistachios in the kitchen in the 2900 block of Alpenglow Way. The bear entered through a screen window in the living room and did not want to leave. Officers used nonlethal methods to scare the bear. It jumped through another window and left.

• • • • • • • • • • • • • • • •

July 30

5:14 a.m. Officers were called to a report of a man who was leaving for work and found a woman sleeping in his car in the 300 block of 12th Street. The woman was in town for a wedding, had too much to drink and decided to sleep in the car. The owner of the car did not want to pursue charges against the woman.

• • • • • • • • • • • • • • • •

Aug. 10

3:39 p.m. Officers were called to a report of a man with a pit bull being approached by another man with a pit bull wanting their dogs to fight. When the man refused, the other man asked if he wanted to fight instead. The police were called, and the man trying to instigate the fights was gone when officers arrived.

• • • • • • • • • • • • • • • •

Aug. 15

11:20 a.m. Officers were called to a report of a suspicious incident in the 1400 block of Morgan Court. A male was pointing some sort of gun up a tree, and someone told the male that he better not be shooting animals, and he ran away.

• • • • • • • • • • • • • • • •

Aug. 18

3:07 a.m. Officers were called to a report of a bear at a hotel in the 1000 block of Walton Creek Road. The man who called police said the bear was the angriest bear he had ever seen and the animal was growling at him. The bear was gone when officers arrived.

Aug. 19

10:06 a.m. Officers were called to a report that someone smeared bear poop on a car and wrote an expletive in the 500 block of Seventh Street.

• • • • • • • • • • • • • • • •

Aug. 21

2:57 p.m. Officers were called to a report of a suspicious incident in the 400 block of Sixth Street. A man came home and discovered his front door was open, and a radio belonging to the Steamboat Springs School District was in the rose bushes. Nothing was missing from the home.

• • • • • • • • • • • • • • • •

Sept. 2

9:03 p.m. Officers were called to a report of a man in his 20s who was "just acting crazy" and jumping in and out of trash cans in the 700 block of Lincoln Avenue. He was found and taken to detox.

• • • • • • • • • • • • • • • •

Sept. 10

5:56 p.m. Officers were called to a report of a suspicious person at Eighth Street and Lincoln Avenue. A man reportedly was dancing on the corner and looked like he was on drugs. He was seen dancing on a bench, and someone picked him up in a car. Officers could not locate him.

• • • • • • • • • • • • • • • •

Sept. 17

8:18 p.m. Officers were called to a report of a dispute between neighbors in the 1700 block of Steamboat Boulevard that may have involved beer being poured into a gas tank.

• • • • • • • • • • • • • • • •

Sept. 18

12:10 a.m. Officers were called to a report of a bear in a Dumpster in the 700 block of Walton Pond Circle. A resident reportedly was wanting to have the bear removed and had wanted to trap the bear. The resident was told not to try to trap bears.

Sept. 18

5:25 p.m. Officers were called to a report of missing sod in the 600 block of Meadowbrook Circle. Neighbors were not getting along, and it was suspected one of the neighbors had moved some of the sod to his property.

• • • • • • • • • • • • • • • •

Sept. 24

8:45 a.m. Officers were called to a report of a suspicious note found on a recycling bin at the base of Steamboat Ski Area that stated, "If you don't want to be contaminated, don't open this container." Feces were found inside the bin, which had been sitting in the sun for a couple of days.

• • • • • • • • • • • • • • • •

Oct. 1

11:10 a.m. Officers were called to a report of a representative from a car security company who said a panic button had been pressed on a car at Fourth Street and Lincoln Avenue. The representative could hear a dog barking in the car. Police think the dog pushed the panic button.

• • • • • • • • • • • • • • • •

Oct. 6

1:05 a.m. Steamboat Springs Police Department officers contacted a suspicious car at Howelsen Hill. A male and female were inside. They said they were just talking.

• • • • • • • • • • • • • • • •

Oct. 13

7:41 a.m. Steamboat Springs Police Department officers were called to a report of an elk carcass stolen from the back of a pickup in the 700 block of South Lincoln Avenue. The elk was found in the area chewed up. It looked like a bear stole the elk.

Oct. 13

6:49 p.m. Officers were called to a report of a woman who was bitten by a cat in the 100 block of Missouri Avenue. The woman was taking her trash out and found a large black cat on a chair in the mudroom. The cat then reportedly jumped off the chair and attacked her.

• • • • • • • • • • • • • • • •

Oct. 15

6:16 a.m. Officers were called to a report of two bear cubs trapped in a Dumpster behind a sandwich shop in the 600 block of Lincoln Avenue. Officers put a wooden board down into the Dumpster to act as a ramp, and the bears were able to climb out.

June 24

6:11 p.m. Officers were called to a report of criminal mischief in the 400 block of Tamarack Drive. A drunken woman who had been released from jail four hours before reportedly threw a neighbor's grill off the balcony. The 55-year-old woman was arrested on suspicion of second-degree tampering and violation of a protection order because she was not supposed to be drinking.

Oct. 19

6:43 a.m. Officers saw a man in his boxers leaning inside the passenger side of a vehicle parked at Village Lane and Merritt Street. The man told police he was getting his wife's birthday present out of the vehicle before she woke up so he could surprise her. While the man was getting the present, the wife woke up and turned on a bedroom light.

3:31 p.m. Officers were called to a report of five people smoking marijuana and drinking beer near the Yampa River. Police contacted the people. They weren't smoking anything at all, and the beer turned out to be root beer.

. . . .

Nov. 6

6:04 p.m. Officers were called to a report of a burglary in the 2700 block of Eagleridge Drive. A woman was walking her dog and noticed feet sticking out of her car. The woman found a man passed out in her car. The man apologized to the woman, and he walked away with a handful of change. About $10 was missing, and the man could not be located.

Nov. 12

4:34 p.m. Routt County Sheriff's Office deputies were called to a report of a person who wanted to know if it was legal for his or her neighbor to have a cannon in the yard at Catamount.

. . . .

Nov. 19

10:57 a.m. Officers were called to a report of 40 pounds of processed venison meat stolen from the bed of someone's pickup in the 1900 block of Ski Time Square Drive.

. . . .

Nov. 24

7:32 p.m. Deputies were called to a report of an assault in the 57500 block of Golden Tide Place in Clark. Two brothers had an argument about chores, and they got into a fight. One brother had a small cut on his back, and the other had red marks and a small cut on his back. The brothers did not want to press charges against each other. One of them left for the night.

Sept. 18

11:53 p.m. Officers were called to check on the welfare of a man in the 400 block of Ore House Plaza. Officers contacted a man who was sleeping in a sleeping bag on a grassy hillside. The man said his car had broken down on U.S. Highway 40, and he had gotten a ride into town. He did not have money for a hotel room and had to wait until the next morning to get parts to repair his car. Police advised the man that it was not a good place to sleep because there were bears in the area. As police were explaining this to the man, a bear came out of the bushes about 20 feet away. The man realized this was not a good place to sleep.

12:28 a.m. Officers were called to a report of a disturbance at a bar in the 600 block of Lincoln Avenue. People who dressed up as gorillas for Halloween were on horseback outside of the bar, causing problems at the entrance. The bar manager asked them to leave.

Nov. 1

Nov. 24

9:27 p.m. Officers were called to a report of two women not getting along in the 2900 block of Burgess Creek Road. One of the women thought the other one was wearing her shirt. They owned the same shirt.

Nov. 27

7:20 a.m. Officers were called to a report of an elderly man who had heavy snow pushed into his driveway. Officers helped dig out the driveway.

Dec. 12

8:41 a.m. Officers were called to a report of threats in the 3100 block of Heavenly View. A resident was upset because someone left a bag of dog waste on a trail. Words were exchanged between the people involved.

Dec. 15

10:42 p.m. Officers were called to a report of a suspicious incident at a hotel in the 3100 block of Ingles Lane. People who were not guests at the hotel were using the pool. The people thought a relative was staying at the hotel, but the relative actually was staying at a different hotel.

Dec. 23

8:27 p.m. Officers were called to a report of a suspicious person in the 400 block of Oak Street. A transient woman was knocking on someone's door asking to use the restroom. Officers gave the woman a voucher for a room for the night.

Dec. 24

8:59 p.m. Officers were called to a report of a person who thought someone was cutting down a Christmas tree along a trail near Fish Creek Falls Road. The person was decorating the tree.

Dec. 28

6:41 p.m. Officers were called to a report of a man who was skiing in the middle of the road at River Queen Lane and Clubhouse Drive. The man was gone when police arrived.

Dec. 29

2:12 p.m. A 27-year-old man came to the police department wanting a hotel voucher. The man said his family locked him out of the house because he had been smoking marijuana.

Dec. 31

10:05 p.m. Officers were called to check on the welfare of a man who was acting suspicious and screaming while holding a long metal rod in the 1800 block of Central Park Drive. Police said the man was upset and frustrated because he was having a hard time putting on a knee brace. The metal rod he was holding was part of the brace.

Testimonials

"Laugh out loud funny. Couldn't possibly be true, but every one of these vignettes actually happened. Only in the glorious town of Steamboat Springs could police be called to such ridiculous service!"

— Ron Krall, owner of Off the Beaten Path bookstore

"A couple of grown men can't even have a trampoline party without the neighbors getting their panties in a bunch."

— Bryant Pugh, subject of Aug. 29, 2013, police blotter entry

"A cop's life is full of crazy, unpredictably dangerous and humorous scenarios, which often lead to uncontrollable feelings of fear, anger, thoughts of complete disbelief and sometimes uncontrollable laughter causing bladder retention failure."

— Garrett Wiggins, Routt County sheriff

"It was a no-brainer to have 'Ski Town Shenanigans' as my go-to coffee table book. Its compact size is perfect for my hobbit house and a true icebreaker for guests not used to conversing in confined spaces."

— Marty Gilligan, unemployed, part-time Steamboat Springs hobbit house co-renter

"The thing I miss the most about being a cop in Steamboat is not knowing whether I'm going to catch a bear from a tree or give directions to someone driving a Mercedes who is lost and trying to find a hippie festival."

— Jeff LaRoche, former Steamboat Springs police officer,
owner of Cantina restaurant and co-owner of E3 Chophouse